Surely the reformed Christian faith as reformed faith is not only reformed, but always reforming - *Semper Reformanda* (as the author points out in his introduction). This book, by a young, creative, challenging writer, exemplifies this aspect of the reformed faith with solid skill and genuine humility. Those inside and outside the "young, restless and reformed" community will profit from this insider's insights. He's learned lots of lessons over the years and shares them with us all. Now we can all read, learn, and live in much better ways as a result.

– DAVID NAUGLE, professor of philosophy, distinguished university professor, Dallas Baptist University and author of *Philosophy: A Student's Guide* (Crossway 2012).

Kyle Worley has given us a profound and personal contribution to understanding the "New Calvinism" of which he is an important part. The book brims over with theological and historical depth, yet comes from Kyle's affections (in the Edwardsian sense) which are stirred by the Lord he serves. Kyle's pastor-father taught him from a young age that "deep theology will lead to deep doxology." All of us concerned that this be the mark of our lives and our churches will be glad for Kyle's zeal for and description of this model of ministry.

– DR. JOSEPH "SKIP" RYAN, Chancellor, Redeemer Seminary, Dallas, Austin, Houston

Pitfalls

ALONG THE PATH TO YOUNG AND REFORMED

Pitfalls

ALONG THE PATH TO YOUNG AND REFORMED

Kyle Worley

Contents

Acknowledgements   xi

Introduction   1

Excursus: What is Reformed Theology?   9

Justification by Orthodoxy   19

Fleeing from the Affections   37

A "Runaway" Reformation   53

The Precious Few   69

Surrogate Christianity   85

God in a Straitjacket?   97

Conclusion   113

Acknowledgments

My inspiration for writing this book was that I wanted to write a book that somebody should have given me my freshman year of college. It was in that pivotal year that I was exposed to Reformed Theology, and I began attending a church populated by many in the young and reformed movement.

I hurt people. I was in love with arguments. My love for Christ was dwindling while my mind was being filled with wonderful information. My sinfulness twisted wonderful things meant to demonstrate my desperation for grace into means for self-exaltation.

As you read ahead, please keep in mind that I dare not speak for everyone everywhere, but merely hope to draw attention to pitfalls that I think many among the young and reformed have stumbled into. I want us to see these pitfalls, and then look to Christ, who is our great hope!

I hope you will join me in this journey.

I have never done anything original in my life. I am incapable of producing anything that does not bear the smudged fingerprints of countless people who helped to form my thoughts and me.

I stand on the shoulders of a long line of godly men and women who have been faithful to serve me and point me to Christ. These people have not asked for any recognition, but I intend to show honor to them as I am called by scripture to do.

"Blessed be the God and Father of our Lord Jesus Christ, who has blessed us in Christ with every spiritual blessing in the heavenly places..." (Eph. 1:3).

I would like to thank:

My wife Lauren. She is my tender warrior, always willing to stand up for God's truth and to support of her husband. I love her dearly and praise Christ that He saw fit to entrust to me such a precious gift.

My wonderful parents, Joseph and Cheryl Worley, who have demonstrated to me faithful devotion to the Lord, faithfulness in marriage, and faithfulness in ministry. What I know, I learned from you.

My brother Tanner, who is my most loyal friend.

My loving church family at First Baptist Church of Groves. Your support and care for me and my family has been an excellent picture of the love of Christ. May we continue to strive together for the sake of the Gospel!

Dr. David Naugle and Dr. Skip Ryan. These men have been more than professors—they have been mentors. Whether in Big Stone Gap lectures at Dr. Naugle's house, or trips to-and-from the airport with Skip, God has used these men to guide me in writing this book and in shaping my pursuit of Christ.

The countless friends and family who financially supported me: Grandma (Pat Grayson), Jessica Mooney, Aunt Susie, Bryan and Alyssa Stiglets, Aaron and Sarah Ross, Bryan Dusek, James and Melissa Moore, and so many others.

I am so thankful for my dear friends Austin Miller and Adam Rosseau, who have probably read this book more times than I have. The guys at Lucid, specifically Brad Bevers, have been so patient and gracious with me. If you are a young author looking to connect with men who love the Lord and hope to produce quality publications for His glory, go see the guys at Lucid.

Introduction

Congenital insensitivity to pain with anhidrosis.

This is an incredibly rare disease in which a person cannot feel pain. I know what you're thinking. "This is amazing. It's the Superhero disease." You're thinking, "How can I contract this disease? Wouldn't it be amazing to not feel pain? I could be the greatest UFC fighter in history."

But this disease is incredibly deadly.

This is because insensitivity to pain does not prevent the damage done to the body during physical trauma. Children who suffer from this disease commonly bite off their tongue, have major infections, are at a higher risk of more severe diseases—all because they cannot feel pain.

I do not have congenital insensitivity to pain, but I do have a disease that often acts and reacts in the same way: sin. The sin that plagues my whole person twists, hardens, and manipulates the desire for eternity that is in my heart (Eccl. 3:11), deceiving it into attempting to satisfy itself with worthless endeavors. This disease is so crafty and deadly that it takes things that God has meant for His glory and my joy and twists them into opportunities for me to serve and praise myself.

Like insensitivity to pain, there is a naïve attraction to sin, not knowing it's deadly consequences.

Sin perverts:
- Sex
- Love
- Relationships
- Worship
- Theology
- All of Life

Yes, even worship and theology can be manipulated and twisted by sin. This is the very thing discussed throughout the course of this book: the devastating effects of sin on the God-glorifying, Christ-exalting theology of the young and reformed.

By way of introduction, let me tell you a bit about myself.

Life

Like Paul in Philippians 3:4-6, if anyone else has confidence in his orthodox upbringing, I have more: baptized by immersion in my 8th year in a Southern Baptist Church, of the people of reformation protestants, of the tribe of Spurgeon Baptists, a Calvinist of Calvinists. As for my theology, Reformed; as for worship and practice, Baptist; as for orthodoxy, as close as could be (revision of Philippians 3:4-6).

All kidding aside, I was raised in the worship and reverence of our great God and King. I have heard horror stories from the children of pastors regarding how the church ran their father out or how the local church destroyed their family, but I don't have any stories like that.

I was raised, and now serve as a student pastor, in a medium-sized Baptist church where the people love the Lord, desire to worship Him fully, and make Him known widely. They are as sweet as a church can possibly be to my parents and brother, and they have supported me through my education. I was raised in

Southeast Texas, and I received my undergraduate degree from Dallas Baptist University in Biblical Studies and Philosophy. I am currently a student both at Redeemer Seminary, where I am working on my Masters of Divinity, as well as Southwestern Seminary, where I am working on a Masters of Arts in Biblical Studies. I am married to a beautiful young woman named Lauren. She is an absolute gift from God, and I praise Christ for His blessing me with her.

I am 22 years old. I have no PhD, little wisdom, and an incredible amount of pride.

So, read ahead with caution.

I had the idea for this book as soon as I graduated from DBU. I had spent four years in a melting pot of young, evangelical, reformed thinkers and had joined the ranks of what has now been called by Colin Hansen *Young, Restless, and Reformed.*[1] I sat under the teaching and pastoral leadership of a church that had a strong reformed flavor. It was a small church in Dallas led by a young, unknown pastor. The name of the church was The Village...you have probably never heard of it. Anyways, I digress. While in university at Dallas Baptist, I fell into many traps that my indwelling sin and the Enemy used to distract me from the Christ-exalting story and mission of the Bible. Some of these pitfalls were found in my romantic life and others in my discipline, but the most were found in my devotional life.

In this book, I have focused my attention on six pitfalls of the young and reformed movement. I only know these pitfalls exist because my whole being bears the countless scars that only a heavy mixture of pride, dogmatism, and deception can cause. But glory be to our Savior Jesus, who has rescued me and continues to rescue me from the struggles, temptations, and sufferings of this present evil age.(Gal. 1:4).

---

[1] Collin Hansen, *Young, Restless, Reformed: A Journalist's Journey with the New Calvinists*, (Wheaton, Ill.: Crossway Books, 2008).

"The Church Reformed and Always Reforming."

Reformation is both a noun and a verb. If you are confused with the word "reformed, fear not. We will spend a whole section immediately following the introduction defining the word "reformed."

Reformed is not a static, placid title, but the name of a position that is constantly holding itself up to the Word of God in an attempt to see wrinkles, imperfections, and failures. I appreciate and agree with Carl Trueman's short definition, "the reformation represents a move to place God as he has revealed himself in Christ at the center of the church's life and thought."[2]

The Reformation was a time period that took place in Europe, primarily Germany, the Netherlands, and Britain that resulted in an evaluation of the state of the Christian faith. The Reformation sought to call the church of God to return to biblical truth. The word "Reformed" as we will be using it throughout this book comes from a particular theological heritage.

From the Reformation emerged what have been called the *Solas* of the reformation. *Sola* is the Latin word meaning "alone." The five *Solas* are:

Sola Scriptura, meaning "Scripture Alone"
Sola Gratia, meaning "Grace Alone"
Sola Fide, meaning "Faith Alone"
Solus Christus, meaning "Christ Alone"
Soli Deo Gloria, meaning "the glory of God alone"

---

[2] Carl Trueman, *Reformation: Yesterday, Today and Tomorrow*, (Ross-shire, Scotland: Christian Focus, 2011), 17.

These *Solas* really captured the main thrust of the reformation which was this: that the Bible is the standard of God's truth about all of life, and that the Bible tells us that God is a gracious God who alone can save humans from their sin and its consequences, which He does when men place their faith in Christ, all of which is for the glory of God alone (Eph. 6). Do you find yourself confused, or would like more information, concerning the idea of Reformed and Reformed theology? After the introduction, we will spend a full chapter giving a brief overview of Reformed theology.

In the current movement of the young and reformed, we see that the word "reformed" has become synonymous with Calvinism. These two words are not synonyms because Calvinism emerged out of the greater reformed movement. Even more specifically, *reformed* has come to be used for those who have been influenced by reformation theology through current Christian leaders like John Piper, JI Packer, John Macarthur, RC Sproul, Al Mohler, CJ Mahaney, Mark Driscoll, and Matt Chandler. Countless other Christian leaders have been influenced by reformed theology. They have taken these great truths and communicated them in a way where many Christians have been persuaded that these truths help to make sense of God's Word and how we are to live.

Reformed is a secondary distinction. The primary title of those who profess Christ as Lord and Savior, and worship Him as such, is Christian. Let's look at it another way.

When dealing with computers, there are two main components to their operation: the hardware and the software. The hardware is the constructed machine. It is the driving force behind the computer. Without the hardware, you have no computer. The software is the operating equipment for the hardware. It accesses all of the potential power of the computer and formats the pieces to where they can be used to get on the Internet, play music, and work efficiently.

In regards to the Christian faith, the Word of God, our salvation, and the gifts of the Holy Spirit are the hardware that God equips each and every member of his church with in order to bring them into the family of God, prepare them for ministry, and equip them with their distinctive gifts and callings. The software of the Christian faith is comprised of many things, but one thing in particular stands out: theological traditions. We all come to the Word of God with glasses on. Whether it is our denominational affiliation or our theological tradition, we bring software with us to the hardware of the Christian faith. Reformed theology is a great piece of Christian software, never replacing the hardware of biblical Christianity, only exalting it.

Like anyone who has downloaded music illegally or streamed viral videos and gotten a computer virus, sometimes the software can be taken control of by a malicious agent and used to destroy the beauty, power, and simple efficiency of the hardware. The poison of sin runs so deep that it can take a theological quest to glorify God and make Him known and corrupt man's interpretation and application of these wonderful truths. This has absolutely nothing to do with the makeup of Reformed theology, but it has everything to do with the indwelling sin of pride rising up within the heart of man.

I have identified 6 pitfalls that could be detrimental to those in the young and reformed movement. There are countless other ways that sin and the Enemy have attempted to fracture the lush theological, Christ-centered landscape of Reformed theology, but being limited by my age and experience, I will have to leave that investigation to one who has walked farther than I have.

The 6 Pitfalls:
1. Justification by Orthodoxy
2. Fleeing from the Affections

3. A Runaway Reformation
4. Gnostic Knowledge
5. Surrogate Christianity
6. God in a Straitjacket

We will spend a good amount of time examining each one of these pitfalls and prayerfully analyzing how each is trying to accomplish a good thing but falls short of their intended target.

In *Creation Regained,* Al Wolters argues, "The task of the Christian is to discern structure and direction. As we have noted, structure denotes the 'essence' of a creaturely thing, the kind of creature it is by virtue of God's creational law. Direction, by contrast, refers to a sinful deviation from that structural ordinance and renewed conformity to it in Christ." [3] Reformed theology has, at its core, the desire to honor and glorify our great God who has accomplished a great work for sinners in Jesus Christ. The problem is that sin has bent the direction of our minds and hearts. What God has created for His glory, the pursuit of knowing God for who He is and what He has done, becomes a platform for our arrogance.

In each of these pitfalls, there will be something good, and the temptation will be to throw it out to solve the problem. The problem is not with orthodoxy, knowledge, imitation, or sovereignty but with the direction that our sinful hearts take these wonderful gifts of God. The hope is that what lies ahead in these chapters will not just be a warning but a pathway out of these pitfalls that brings us to a place where we can be agents of restoration within this young and reformed movement.

To come to a place of honesty with ourselves regarding some the immaturities and weaknesses in the midst of this movement allows us to practice one of the great mottos of the

[3] Albert Wolters, *Creation Regained: Biblical Basics for a Reformational Worldview,* (2nd ed. Grand Rapids, Mich.: William B. Eerdmans Pub., 2005), 88.

Reformation: *Semper Reformanda*, meaning, "always reforming." John MacArthur said it well when he reminded us that, "no one is truly reformed who is not constantly reforming."[4]

What do we mean when we use the word "reformed?" Let's take a look.

---

[4] MacArthur, John. "Grow Up. Settle Down. Keep Reforming." Grace To You. http://www.gty.org/blog/B110720 (accessed August 24, 2012).

Excursus:
What is Reformed Theology?

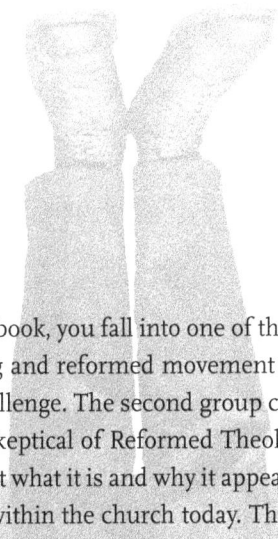

If you bought this book, you fall into one of three groups. The first group is the young and reformed movement that I am writing to encourage and challenge. The second group consists of those who are interested or skeptical of Reformed Theology and are seeking to learn more about what it is and why it appears to be a huge piece of the discussion within the church today. The last group is made up of those who happened to buy this book because they knew my name, liked the cover, or recognized one of the endorsements on the back of the book.

I want to take a brief detour at the beginning of this book to get us all on the same page regarding a key component in the scope of this book: Reformed Theology. Many in the first group will recognize and understand in some respect the content and goal of Reformed Theology. Those who are in the second and third group may not know what I mean when I say that we will be discussing Reformed Theology, so I would like to spend a few pages establishing a basic understanding of what it means to have a reformed perspective on God and His Word.

I would like to quote Trueman's definition again, "The reformation represents a move to place God as he has revealed himself in Christ at the centre of the church's life and thought."[1]

---

[1] Carl Trueman, *Reformation: Yesterday, Today and Tomorrow*, (Ross-shire, Scotland: Christian Focus, 2011), 17.

He is speaking of the Reformation as a historical period wherein church leaders such as Wycliffe (1328-1384), Luther (1483-1546), Zwingli (1484-1531), Hus (1369-1415), Calvin (1509-1564), Beza (1519-1605), and many others worked to restore the church's focus to the work of God in Christ as revealed in the Word of God. For the church and its leaders to accomplish this task, they had to assert a theological foundation that affirmed the central place God's Word holds in revealing the gracious work of God on our behalf in the person of Christ Jesus.

Resting on Trueman's definition of the Reformation, we can confidently say that Reformed Theology calls the church to hold itself to the authority of God's Word by trusting in the saving grace of God, which is applied by the Holy Spirit in the gift of faith in Christ alone for the glory of God alone.

I would like to now take a moment to answer a few questions you might have. Please understand that I cannot be exhaustive and will conclude this section with book recommendations that will assist you in any further study you might be interested in doing concerning reformed theology.

"What Are Key Beliefs in Reformed Theology?"

While we don't have the time to run through the Reformed perspective on every doctrine, it is important to list a few distinctive truths of Reformed Theology.

The centrality of God's Word: We mentioned in the introduction that the reformers placed a strong emphasis on the Word of God. The principle of *sola scriptura* guided the reformers in their quest to submit all of life to the will of God as expressed in God's Word. 2 Timothy 3:16 says, "All scripture is breathed out by God." If we have the very words of God, they demand to be the standard by which everything claiming to be good, true, or beautiful is judged.

The sovereignty of God: God is the universe's creator and sustainer. He is eternal, and He possesses complete governing authority over His creatures. The *1689 London Baptist Confession* states that God has "most sovereign dominion over all creatures, to do by them, for them, or upon them, whatsoever Himself pleases."[2] In regards to salvation, Reformed Theology places a high emphasis on the electing or predestinating work of God on behalf of sinners. The Old Testament is the story of God's work of setting apart a people who would be committed to the worship of God. Like Paul says in Romans 11:36, "For from him and through him and to him are all things. To him be glory forever. Amen."

The sinfulness of man: Man is born broken in sin. Psalm 51 says, "I was brought forth in iniquity, and in sin did my mother conceive me." The natural state of humanity is depicted by Paul in Ephesians 2:1-2 as "dead in the trespasses and sins in which [we] once walked." We are unable and unwilling to choose righteousness apart from the gracious work of God in us.

Salvation by faith alone in Christ alone: One of the key truths that regained proper attention during the Reformation was the biblical truth that salvation was by faith alone in Christ alone. The Catholic Church had communicated to the people, whether intentionally or unintentionally, that salvation was obtained through a works-based system. In Romans 5:1-2, Paul says, "Therefore, since we have been justified by faith, we have peace with God through our Lord Jesus Christ. Through him we have also obtained access by faith into this grace in which we stand, and we rejoice in hope of the glory of God." What a glorious

---

[2] Peter Masters, *The Baptist Confession of Faith 1689, or, The Second London Confession: With Scripture Proofs,* (London: Wakeman Trust, 1998), Part 2, Chapter 2.

truth! In Ephesians 2 we see that God gives the gift of faith and then directs us to the person of Christ where we receive the salvation He has secured on our behalf.

"Is Reformed Theology New?"

Reformed Theology is not new. Many of the wonderful truths that are held in high regard among the young and reformed today were on the lips of early church fathers.

More than that, one of the primary tasks of the Reformation was to lift up the Word of God as the final authority on matters of doctrine and worship. That being said, Reformed Theology seeks to be biblical. When you read the work of Luther, Calvin, Beza, Knox, or Owen, you will find countless quotations of the early church fathers. Calvin quotes Augustine so often that in some sections you almost feel as if you are reading the man himself. As much as these men quote and make use of the early church fathers, their use of scripture overwhelms any other source. The Reformers sought to be people of the Book.

2 Timothy 3:16 tells us that, "All scripture is breathed out by God and profitable for teaching, for reproof, for correction, and for training in righteousness, that the man of God may be complete, equipped for every good work." Reformed theologians take this passage and hold it up, among many others, to demonstrate the inspiration, authority, and sufficiency of scripture.

Since Reformed Theology places a high emphasis on the authority of scripture, it tends to be argued for from the basis of scripture. The scriptural foundation for the key doctrines in Reformed Theology finds support in the voices of early church fathers like Gregory of Nazianzus (AD 330-390), Athanasius (AD 296-373), and Augustine (AD 354-430). When reading these early church leaders, we will often hear emphasis placed on truths that would receive a renewed focus a thousand years later in the Reformation.

"Who is Reformed?"

Reformed Theology cannot be boiled down to one denomination, church, or church leader. Some will speak as if all of Reformed Theology can be expressed in the work of John Calvin; this simply is not true. Others will suggest that Reformed Theology is for the Presbyterians, but this also is merely one branch of the Reformed tree.

So what am I taking to be the standard for what I call Reformed? I am taking the *Westminster Confession of Faith*,[3] The *Three forms of Unity*,[4] and *The 1689 London Confession*.[5] These confessions and catechisms are not in complete unity, but they express the various trajectories that were consistent with the Solas of the Reformation, mentioned in the introduction, and the governing project to hold the church up to the Word of God in matters of doctrine and devotion.

I will also be using examples from church leaders across the history of the church to demonstrate the breadth of reformed theology. We will hear from Charles Spurgeon, John Calvin, Augustine, Luther, Edwards, and John Knox throughout the course of this book.

Within Reformed Theology are many "family discussions" that would distinguish specific branches of the Reformed tradition. Without a doubt, one can argue that if you are a

---

[3] G. I. Williamson, *The Westminster Confession of Faith for Study Classes*, (2nd ed. Phillipsburg, N.J.: P & R Pub., 2004).

[4] Joel Beeke, *The Three Forms of Unity: Heidelberg Catechism, Belgic Confession, Canons of Dort*, (Birmingham, AL: Solid Ground Christian Books, 2010).

[5] Peter Masters, *The Baptist Confession of Faith 1689, or, The Second London Confession: With Scripture Proofs*, (London: Wakeman Trust, 1998).

member of any protestant (non-Roman Catholic) church, your denomination has been influenced by the theology that was made explicit in the Reformation.

"Does Reformed Mean Calvinist?"

In the young and reformed movement, there has been some confusion between the terms Calvinist and Reformed. John Calvin was a prominent figure in the Reformation, but he was not the only leader around. Calvin has received a renewed focus as the "five points of Calvinism" have become a litmus test for those who claim to be among the young and reformed. Sadly, Calvin's work was much greater than the "five points" seem to indicate.

We should see Calvin and his theological heritage, Calvinism, as a major influence during the Reformation and as a piece of what we call Reformed Theology, but to reduce it to Calvinism is harmful for 3 reasons.

First, Calvin was one among many. Although Time magazine called the "new Calvinism" one of the top ten ideas that are changing the world,[6] we must be careful that we don't reduce the rich theological heritage of the Reformation. Calvin was definitely an influential figure in the Reformation, but for all that Calvin offers, if he were the only leader who's work affected the young and reformed movement, we would be in a poor condition.

Take for example Luther's emphasis on justification by faith alone. Luther emphasizes that we are made right with God by the work of God on our behalf in Jesus Christ as the sacrifice for sins. Calvin would hold to the doctrine of justification by faith alone as well, but union with Christ is much more integral to

---

[6] David Van Biema, "The New Calvinism - 10 Ideas Changing the World Right Now - TIME."

his theological system. Union with Christ reminds us that Christ is in us and we are in Christ. J. Todd Billings has wonderfully demonstrated that union with Christ is "not an afterthought for Calvin but provides the basic imagery and structure for key motifs in his doctrine of salvation."[7] In the words of Phil Ryken, "Calvin's theology turns on the spiritual reality of being in Christ."[8] If we had Luther's doctrine of justification without Calvin's doctrine of union, we would be lacking in our overall understanding of scripture. We need to see Reformed Theology as encompassing a greater work than merely that of John Calvin.

Secondly, Calvin is not infallible. Calvin is but a man. After Isaiah compares flesh with grass, he says, "The grass withers, the flower fades, but the word of our God will stand forever" (Is. 40:8). To be truly reformed means to lift up the Word of God and to examine any truth claim in its light. If we were caught claiming the authority of Calvin, Calvin himself would rebuke us and remind us that we are all subject to the authority of God's Word. Calvin's thought is debated and discussed in such a way as to demonstrate that even Calvinists don't agree on Calvin's work.

Finally, many among the young and reformed are getting secondhand Calvin. For all the discussion regarding John Calvin and Calvinism, it appears that many among the young and reformed profess to be "Calvinist" because their favorite leaders, preachers, or authors claim to be Calvinists. It often becomes apparent when the young and reformed speak of Calvinism that they are speaking of what are called the "Five Points" of Calvinism. These "Five Points"—total depravity, unconditional election, limited atonement, irresistible grace, and perseverance of the saints—emerged after Calvin died to combat the errors

---

[7] J. Todd Billings, *Union With Christ: Reframing Theology and Ministry for the Church*, (Grand Rapids, Mich.: Baker Academic, 2011), Ch. 3, Section1, para. 4.

[8] Phil Ryken, "The Believer's Union with Christ," *John Calvin: A Heart for Devotion, Doctrine & Doxology*, (Lake Mary, FL: Reformation Trust, 2008), 192.

of Arminianism. The man would have been offended to have a theological system branded with his name. That is not to say that the "five points" of Calvinism do not have their roots in Calvin's work; it just demonstrates that historical perspective is not a strong suit of the young and reformed. We need to grow in a deep appreciation and awareness of our heritage; all of it, not merely the work of one man.

We will talk more about Calvin's life, theology, and ministry in the chapter entitled "The Precious Few."

"Why Should I Care About Reformed Theology?"

In J.I. Packer's introductory essay to the *Death of Death in the Death of Christ* by John Owen, Packer says some preliminary words about Calvinism. As I have suggested, reformed theology is not synonymous with Calvinism, but Packer's words in this essay are a fitting description for the scope of reformed theology.

Packer says, "Calvinism [read reformed theology] is a world-view, stemming from a clear vision of God as the whole world's Maker and King. Calvinism is the consistent endeavor to acknowledge the Creator as the Lord, working all things after the counsel of His will. Calvinism is a theocentric way of thinking about all life under the direction and control of God's own word."[9]

Reformed Theology creates a reformational worldview. A worldview is just a big name for the lens through which we view the world. Everyone has a set of lenses; everyone has a worldview. When we dig into Reformed Theology, we find ourselves beginning to look at the entire world through reformational lenses. As Packer says, "We acknowledge the Creator as the Lord,

---

[9] John Owen and J.I. Packer, *The Death of Death in the Death of Christ.* (Edinburgh: Banner of Truth Trust, 1983), 5.

working all things after the counsel of His will."[10] Implicit in this idea is that God is not detached from His creation. God is saving, reconciling, restoring and leading the world to His desired end.

You should care about Reformed Theology because it helps to lay a foundation that provides Christians with a deep narrative structure from which we can discern the truth, beauty, and good in the midst of this broken world. Reformed Theology gives us a frame for the wonderful story of the gospel. Unlike many other theological systems, Reformed Theology places a strong emphasis on the worldview that emerges from its claims. You should care about Reformed Theology because as the world continues to grow more comfortable with believing in a god of their own making, Reformed Theology desires to exalt God as He has revealed Himself in His Word.

You should care about Reformed Theology because men and women were persecuted in their effort to return to biblical truth. There is a naïve assumption that is often made regarding the Reformed movement. Many assume that those preachers, theologians, and authors who emerged in the Reformation were merely individuals with too much time on their hands. Some claim that these men developed their theology in "ivory-towers." This claim is often made in an effort to discredit the legitimacy of theological beliefs that were accented during the Reformation. It also could not be further from the truth. Many of the leaders of the Reformation were severely persecuted (imprisoned, exiled, tortured, and killed) for their commitment to biblical truth. We should be grateful that these men and women were willing to suffer for the sake of truth.

You should care about Reformed Theology because there is a movement of people across the Global West that share a renewed interest in the truths proclaimed during the Reformation. For

---

[10] Ibid.

the rest of this book we will spend our time looking at this young and reformed movement, hoping to see the beautiful ways God is working in and through it, while at the same time, realizing the pitfalls that our sin creates along the path.

FURTHER READING

What is Reformed Theology by RC Sproul
Creation Regained by Al Wolters
The Transforming Vision by Richard Middleton and Bryan Walsh

Justification by Orthodoxy

1

"Put no confidence in the mere fact that you hold to an orthodox faith, for a dead orthodoxy soon corrupts."[1]

Justification and Orthodoxy are two great words. They are rich words that bring joy and confidence to the hearts of Christians because of the great work of Christ (justification) and true belief about God (orthodoxy). These two words have received a renewed interest from the young and reformed movement, who care deeply about the work accomplished by Jesus and the truth about who God is and what He has done.

What is justification?[2] Justification is a judicial act of God, in which He declares, on the basis of the righteousness of Jesus Christ, that all the claims of the law are satisfied with respect to the sinner.[3] The truth of justification jumps off the pages when

---

[1] C.H. Spurgeon and Kerry James Allen, *Exploring the mind and heart of the prince of preachers: five-thousand Illustrations selected from the works of Charles Haddon Spurgeon.* (Oswego, IL: Fox River Press, 2005), 332.

[2] I understand that in recent years there has been a debate over the precise view that Paul had regarding justification. My thoughts regarding the view of the law in Palestinian Judaism (a foundational piece to the "New Perspective on Paul" discussion) are in keeping with those found in DA Carson and Peter O'Brien's work *Justification and Variegated Nomism.* I would also recommend John Piper's *The Future of Justification.*

[3] Louis Berkhof, *Systematic theology,* (4th rev. and enl. ed. Grand Rapids, Mich.: W.B. Eerdmans Pub. Co., 1941), 513.

we read passages like Philippians 3:8-9, which says, "Indeed, I count everything as loss because of the surpassing worth of knowing Christ Jesus my Lord. For his sake I have suffered the loss of all things and count them as rubbish, in order that I may gain Christ and be found in him, not having a righteousness of my own that comes from the law, but that which comes through faith in Christ, the righteousness from God that depends on faith..."[4]

This wonderful truth was at the heart of the reformation movement in the 16th century as seen in Martin Luther's famous words, "For if we lose the article of justification, we lose all things together."[5]

When we talk about justification, we are talking about a central truth that concerns us deeply, since it deals with the question of how we are made right before God, by God. A firm belief in justification by faith alone is, and should always be, a test of one's orthodoxy (right belief). **But to make orthodoxy the grounds of your justification is, in fact, not orthodoxy.**

Justification is not some mere theological concept; it is a work accomplished by the God-Man, Jesus Christ. Even though God has accomplished such a great and magnificent work on our behalf, we (everyone who has ever existed) are constantly striving for self-justification. We want to make ourselves right before God because it keeps us independent, autonomous, and in control. We see this clearly in the religious leaders of Jesus' day. The Pharisees were students of scripture, but in their quest to conform all of their beliefs and practices to the standards of scripture, they missed the purpose of scripture. Jesus tells the Pharisees, "You search the Scriptures because you think that in

---

[4] See also: Ro. 3:24-25; Ro. 5:1; 2 Cor. 5:21

[5] Luther, M. (1997). *Commentary on Galatians* (Ga 1:3). Oak Harbor, WA: Logos Research Systems, Inc.

them you have eternal life; and it is they that bear witness about me, yet you refuse to come to me that you may have life" (John 5:39-40). The Pharisees misunderstood the role of orthodoxy.

What is orthodoxy? Orthodoxy is the "sound doctrine" (Titus 2:1) of the church. Orthodoxy also has a historical dimension in that it is the "faith that was once for all delivered to the saints" (Jude 1:3). It has been passed down through God's people from the beginning of the Church until now.

So, shouldn't orthodox theology point to the object of which it speaks?

That's the question we commonly ask about the Jewish religious leaders who saw God incarnate, Jesus, their promised Savior, and yet rejected Him. What blinded their eyes? What consumed them to the point that they crucified Christ as He clarified everything they thought they knew?

The Jewish religious leaders were consumed with complete knowledge and perfect obedience to the Law. This quest for complete knowledge and perfect obedience was at the heart of every Jew in Palestine, and every time Christ walked by and picked grain or healed on the Sabbath, forgave people, or called them a brood of vipers they labeled him an "unorthodox" man. Their quest for orthodoxy, perfect understanding of the law, led them to believe that they could also perfectly obey the law. When we define our righteousness as anything other than the work of Christ on our behalf, we trade God's perfect sacrifice for our attempt at perfection. And we fail. The quest for perfect orthodoxy was never meant to be our means of justification, it was meant to be the means by which we uncover He who makes us right with God.

Christ is the perfect example of orthodoxy, and He is the God who saves us into true Christian orthodoxy. It is only in our twisted and tainted hearts that we take something as pure and inspired as the revelation of God and completely miss the point.

Just like the Pharisees, the temptation for those in the young reformed crowd is to root their salvation in their orthodoxy. They find the hope and promise of their salvation not in what Christ has accomplished as the fulfillment of God's redemptive plan but in their preferred articulation of this great salvation.

There are many among the young and reformed who, like the religious leaders of Christ's day, have moved from justification by faith alone in Christ alone to justification by knowledge alone in the reformed tradition alone. So when you join these two great words, justification and orthodoxy, with the word "by," the result is a dangerous pitfall that many have stumbled into in their quest to glorify God with their pursuit of truth. At the beginning of his book *Desiring God* (required reading for the young and reformed), John Piper quotes from Charles Williams' *The Place of the Lion*: "How accurate must one be with one's prepositions! Perhaps it was a preposition wrong that set the whole world awry."[6] Whenever the beautiful truth of justification is connected to "orthodoxy" with the wrong preposition, we get a dangerous stumbling block that can lead to destruction.

So, what is orthodoxy? What does the quest for orthodoxy look like? Are we righteous because we are orthodox? What is genuine orthodoxy?

Let's take a look.

What is orthodoxy?

Orthodoxy literally means "right opinion," and it is used in Christian theology to refer to what "the New Testament calls 'sound doctrine,' that which rightly reflects in summary form all the teaching of Scripture and which the church is bound to

---

[6] Quoted in John Piper, *Desiring God: Meditations of a Christian Hedonist*, (New expanded ed. Nottingham: Inter-Varsity, 2002), 16.

believe and obey."[7] The idea of orthodoxy has come under attack since the modern period, and this attack has grown stronger in the midst of our current post-modern era.

Orthodoxy has been attacked because of its exclusive nature. If you have orthodoxy, a coherent set of beliefs and truths that are firm and unbending, then you also have heresy, which is anything that contradicts this coherent set of beliefs and truths. The division between what is true (orthodoxy) and what is false (heresy) is not a division that our culture appreciates or respects. To claim that you believe and practice a truth that should be believed and practiced by everyone has been a radical and offensive claim in western culture since the dawn of the 19th century.

This has led many, even some within the Church, to dismiss orthodoxy as a vain attempt to gather a group of people under a governing set of beliefs, or even worse, to claim that any quest for orthodoxy is an act of oppression that seeks to stifle and suppress the individuality of humanity.

Orthodoxy is a term that is often used in reference to Christian theology. Theology is the study of God, and we are all theologians. Everyone who has ever lived or will live is a theologian, the only question is whether he or she is a good theologian or not. A.W. Tozer once said, "what comes into our minds when we think about God is the most important thing about us."[8] We all shape the world in accordance with the way we view and worship God. If our theology is wrong, our lives, loves, and actions will follow suit. That is why orthodoxy—all that is true about who God is and what He has done—is vastly

---

[7] Gregg Allison, *Historical Theology: An Introduction to Christian Doctrine : A Companion to Wayne Grudem's Systematic Theology*, (Grand Rapids, Mich.: Zondervan, 2011), 24.

[8] A. W. Tozer, *The Knowledge of the Holy: The Attributes of God: Their Meaning in the Christian Life*, (New York: HarperSanFrancisco, 1992), 1.

important. Our theology affects all of life, so we should strive to have a sound, or orthodox, theology.

Even though orthodoxy, the "sound doctrine" of the Bible, has recently come under attack, there has been a renewed interest in asking the question, "What is orthodox theology?" Or, "What is true theology?"

One of the virtues of the young and reformed movement is its desire to return to the Word of God being the centerpiece of the life and practice of the church. In so doing, this young movement has been exposed to the deep and profound truths of who God has revealed Himself to be.

Paul writes to a young Christian leader by the name of Titus, challenging him to examine the leaders in the city he is serving by seeing that they "hold firm to the trustworthy word as taught, so that he may be able to give instruction in sound doctrine and also to rebuke those who contradict it" (Titus 1). This verse speaks directly to the controversial nature of orthodoxy. Paul is telling Titus that there is a definite and absolute set of beliefs that your leaders should know, believe, practice, and articulate. Not only should these leaders believe and practice what is true, but they should also be able to identify and rebuke what is false. As believers, we should be able to articulate biblical truth and defend it from those seeking to undermine its foundation.

Many involved in the young and reformed movement grew up in churches that watered down the deep truths of God's Word. Outside of these churches they were confronted with the harsh realities of the world, and they quickly realized that they had been sold a theology that was neither deep nor genuine enough to answer the hard questions of life. So, if orthodoxy is really the collection of biblical truths that govern and bring coherence to God's people, what's wrong with orthodoxy?

The problem is not orthodoxy. The problem is that in our quest for orthodoxy we have made doctrines and theology the answer rather than the signposts pointing us to the God and Savior of whom they speak.

The Quest for Orthodoxy

Maybe like never before, authenticity has become one of the supreme desires of this generation. The emergence of "reality" television, independent music, and coffee shop culture has successfully started this generation on a quest to find and treasure all that is *real* and *authentic*. Our consumer culture has picked up on this and has poised itself for yet another transition—from the glitz and glam of the eighties, the angst and melodrama of the nineties, to the *real* and *gritty* that we currently see on billboards and television.

A pre-occupation with all that claims to be genuine and authentic is mirrored in the current quest for orthodoxy seen among the young and reformed. This is partly because the digital age has opened up endless opportunities to be exposed to Christian leaders who have reflected and learned from Reformation-era theology. Another factor is young people realizing the reality that the church had sold them some practical, often moralistic,[9] advice and called it Christian theology or biblical truth. As these young men and women enter into a new season of their lives, and globalization brings vastly different cultural ideas into their backyards, they are

---

[9] I would like to thank Dr. David Naugle for pointing me to Christian Smith's work regarding what he calls "moralistic therapeutic deism." Smith argues that most of what passes for "Christianity" among emerging adults consists of the idea that there is a god with not much to do other than to give gifts to and console those who live a good life. You can read his work on "moral therapeutic deism" in Christian Smith, Soul Searching: The Religious and Spiritual Lives of American Teenagers, (Oxford: Oxford University Press, 2005) and Christian Smith, Souls in Transition: The Religious and Spiritual Lives of Emerging Adults, (Oxford: Oxford University Press, 2009).

struck by how bland, boring, and fractured their understanding of what they profess to believe has been.

There is no doubt that a quest for orthodoxy is at the heart of the young and reformed movement, although it is often phrased as, "We desire to be biblical..." This quest has issued forth a challenge to church leaders, authors, seminary professors, Sunday school teachers, and many others to return to the Word of God as the source for what we say about who God is and what He has done.

The problem is that this quest for orthodoxy, in its worst forms, has become about winning arguments and stating perfect positions instead of leading people to deeper and richer understandings of God's revelation. When we begin a quest for perfection, regardless of what we are endeavoring to be perfect in, we entering into idolatry. We are called to be biblically faithful and to pursue excellence in our understanding of God's revelation, but to pursue perfection is to indulge the pride of sin. J.I. Packer, at the beginning of his magisterial *Knowing God,* says that before one embarks on diving into the depths of theology they must ask themselves a question: "What is my ultimate aim and object in occupying my mind with these things? What do I intend to do with my knowledge about God, once I have it?"[10]

If orthodoxy is not seen as a means to an end, that end being the worship of Jesus and the mission of His church, then Packer warns, "to be preoccupied with getting theological knowledge as an end in itself, to approach Bible study with no higher a motive than a desire to know all the answers, is the direct route to a state of self satisfied self-deception."[11]

---

[10] J.I. Packer, *Knowing God*, (20th anniversary ed. Downers Grove, Ill.: InterVarsity Press, 1993), 21.

[11] Ibid; 22.

For example, the doctrine of election, a beautiful truth that humbles the human heart with an awareness of the profound love that God bestowed upon His people before the foundations of the world, is twisted into a point of argument between free will and God's sovereignty. Forgetting the worship this truth should lead us to, we settle for an argument from a prideful heart.

There are some who would say, "But Kyle, I worship as I pursue truth." I would say that if pursuing biblical truth leads you to worship the God who has revealed it, then you are pursuing truth for a holy purpose. I fear that much of the pursuit of biblical truth is merely information accumulation for the purposes of argumentation. That pursuit is unholy. Polemics and arguing for biblical truth have a place among the young and reformed, but they cannot be our brand.

Like those who cried for Barabbas when they could have had Jesus, all of those who have joined the ranks of the young and reformed movement must be careful of the pitfall that roots our justification (what makes us right with God) in our orthodoxy. If we are not watchful we may be found engaging in a destructive pursuit that elevates correct opinion about God to the place of true union with God.

The Failure of Justification by Orthodoxy

Why is it destructive to root our justification in our orthodoxy? Why is it destructive to believe we can be made righteous in God's sight solely by the accuracy of our belief about God?

It's destructive to root our justification in anything but the finished work of Jesus Christ because all else is shaking sand. The reason it is so appealing to place our justification in our orthodoxy is because it deceives us into thinking we can be sovereign over our salvation. Even in the young and reformed movement, we sometimes talk about God's sovereignty in a way that implies that unless you fully understand how and why God is sovereign, you can't experience His sovereign grace.

In many young and reformed circles, the fathers of our faith like Noah, Abraham, and Moses would be looked down upon because of the limitedness of their knowledge of the God who had saved them. These men do not give Christians an exemption from meditating and reflecting on the deep truths of who God is and what He has done, but they do place our quest to know God on the foundation of faith instead of knowledge.

Theology affects all of life. If we believe that we can be our own source of justification, then this will not merely affect how we live and practice our Christianity; it will affect how we bring that faith to bear on the life of the world.

Most of us would deny outright that we can justify ourselves, but I would challenge you to look at the content of your faith. Are you primarily concerned about learning more and more facts about God or about knowing God? When you (if you!) bring your faith into conversation with anyone, is it often for the purposes of correcting wrong ideas they have about God? **Do you primarily point people to Jesus or arguments?**

In one of the most influential lectures I have heard, Ray Ortlund argued that the gospel, "and justification in particular, calls for more than doctrinal subscription; it also calls for cultural incarnation."[12] Our theology will "flesh out" in our lives, and we should often reflect on the substance of our faith. Are we desperate for grace or for more knowledge? Are we already putting what we believe into practice? Have you set up an arbitrary standard of knowledge that you must possess before you can begin to share the truth God has already revealed to you with others?

---

[12] Ray Ortlund Jr., "Justification Versus Self-Justification." The Gospel Coalition. thegospelcoalition.org/blogs/rayortlund/files/2011/04/TGClecture.pdf (accessed August 24, 2012), Page 1. Paragraph 2.

Luther, speaking of justification by faith alone, said that, "it cannot be beaten into our ears enough or too much. Yea, though we learn it and understand it well, yet is there none that taketh hold of it perfectly, or believeth it with all his heart. So frail a thing is our flesh, and disobedient to the spirit."[13]

We long for self-justification because it places us in the driver's seat for our salvation. This current young and reformed movement must beware of the self-justification pitfall of rooting what makes us right with God in the accuracy of our knowledge of who God is and what He has done. In this regard, the great reformer John Calvin was prophetic when he warned us that the worst screen to block the power of the Holy Spirit would be a confidence in our own intelligence.

Charles Spurgeon and the Downgrade Controversy

Charles Spurgeon holds a special place in my heart. As a young student, I encountered his sermons and was refreshed by two things that he held close to his heart: Calvinist theology and evangelistic passion.

Spurgeon was a powerhouse preacher in London during the late Victorian period. He led one of the largest churches and was the creator of countless other Christian organizations (a college, orphanages, mission unions). Spurgeon was also a Calvinist. He says in a sermon on election, "I love to proclaim these strong old doctrines, that are called by nickname Calvinism, but which are surely and verily the revealed truth of God as it is in Christ Jesus."[14]

---

[13] Luther, M. (1997). *Commentary on Galatians* (Ga 1:3). Oak Harbor, WA: Logos Research Systems, Inc.

[14] Charles Spurgeon, *Spurgeon's Sermons Volume Two*, (Peabody: Hendrickson, 2011), 69.

Towards the end of Spurgeon's life, Calvinist theology had begun to be exchanged for theology that appeared to be more acceptable to modern man. Higher Criticism, which sounds like a distinguished thing but in all reality is really a nice name for skepticism, had begun to put pastors into pulpits among the Free Churches (Methodists, Baptists, Plymouth Brethren, etc.) that did not believe in the inspiration of God's Word, the deity of Jesus, or the truth that Christ was our substitutionary atonement.

Spurgeon objected to this wholeheartedly. He argued for the Evangelicals (those Protestants united in the gospel) to come together and affirm these core truths. Spurgeon was able to argue for unity because Calvinism had given Spurgeon a unified structure in which to sort and organize the truth of God's Word. During this process, Spurgeon's concern was not primarily to guard the ideas of men, but to guard the truth of God's Word. This was not just for tradition or orthodoxy's sake, but also that the substance of the gospel would not be diluted. The period wherein Spurgeon defended orthodoxy from those who would want to water it down became known as the "Downgrade Controversy" since the idea was to downgrade orthodox theology in an attempt to make it more acceptable.

Spurgeon was not just attacked by those who were trying to undermine orthodoxy but also from those who were seeking to be perfectly orthodox. Hyper-Calvinists of the late Victorian period attacked Spurgeon for not being Calvinist enough.

As Ian Murray has said, "both Hyper-Calvinism and Arminianism took issue with Spurgeon, and strangely enough on the same ground. Spurgeon held, because he believed Scripture teaches it, that man is responsible to believe the gospel, yet on account of sin wholly unable to do so."[15]

---

[15] Iain Murray, *The Forgotten Spurgeon*, (2nd ed. Edinburgh: Banner of Truth Trust, 2009), 8.

Spurgeon was caught in the tension between those who said he was not orthodox enough and others who claimed that he was the voice of an orthodoxy that was dying out. In the midst of this tension, had Spurgeon rooted his justification in his orthodoxy, he would have lacked the boldness and faith required to confidently stand up for truth. Had Spurgeon found what made him right with God in the precision and correctness of his theology, he would never have been able to stand up for this theology during those crucial times.

Lewis Drummond, who has written an expansive biography of the great preacher, has written, "Spurgeon stood fully committed to these doctrines [Calvinism]. But it should be noted that he did not demand that everyone assent to all points as a necessary prerequisite for the experience of redemption itself."[16]

When we see how a man like Spurgeon reacts to crisis, we can see the deep truth that our Savior sustains us, not our theology. Murray says, "it may well be that we have not been sufficiently alert to the danger of allowing a supposed consistency in doctrine to override the biblical priority of zeal for Christ and the souls of men."[17]

When Spurgeon begins his sermon on "Sovereignty and Salvation," he introduces a passage from Isaiah 14:22 that states, "Turn to me and be saved, all the ends of the earth! For I am God, and there is no other." It was the verse spoken by a minister in a little church in the middle of a snowstorm that grabbed Charles Spurgeon's heart. At the core of Spurgeon's orthodoxy was a humility that only comes from experiencing the saving grace of God in Christ Jesus.

---

[16] Lewis Drummond, *Spurgeon: Prince of Preachers*, (Grand Rapids, MI: Kregel Publications, 1992), 635.

[17] Iain Murray, *Spurgeon v. Hyper-Calvinism: The Battle for Gospel Preaching*, (Edinburgh: Banner of Truth Trust, 1995), xiv.

As Spurgeon said, "A man may be evidently of God's chosen family, and yet though elected, may not believe in the doctrine of election. I hold there are many savingly called, who do not believe in effectual calling, and that there are a great many who persevere to the end, who do not believe the doctrine of final perseverance. We do now hope that the hearts of many are a great deal better than their heads."[18]

So let us pursue orthodoxy, but let us walk with a limp. Let us be humble as we pursue biblical truth. We do not stand confidently on our own ability to reason and argue, but we stand assuredly on the person and work of Christ.

A Humble Orthodoxy

"Cage Calvinism" is the name that many call the early stages of a Christian's journey into the reformed tradition. Douglas Wilson says in *Mother Kirk* that there is a cage stage in Calvinism when "the newly convinced Calvinist ought be locked into a cage, and not let out until he stabilizes, or the medication kicks in."[19] This nickname is a good fit for many of those who are young in their exposure to Calvinism. One of the saddest ironies of the doctrines of grace is that sin seems to twist them and create such ungracious adherents.

In Psalm 119 we see the Psalmist rejoicing in God's revelation. In verse 160, the Psalmist writes, "the sum of your word is truth, and every one of your righteous rules endures forever." This sounds like orthodoxy.

When we look at Psalm 119, we hear countless thanksgivings for the truth of God's Word, the eternal nature of the Word of

---

[18] Quoted in Iain Murray, *Spurgeon v. Hyper-Calvinism: the battle for gospel preaching*, (Edinburgh: Banner of Truth Trust, 1995), 112.

[19] Douglas Wilson, *Mother Kirk: Essays and Forays in Practical Ecclesiology*, (Moscow, Idaho: Canon Press, 2001), 88.

God, and the goodness and hope to which it points. However, the Psalmist is not primarily commending the knowledge of God's Word as an end in itself, but the knowledge of God's Word that leads to "walking in the law of the Lord!" (v.1). He says, "blessed are those who keep his testimonies, who seek **him** with their whole heart" (v.2, emphasis mine).

The psalmist was passionate about theology and orthodoxy: right belief about God and the knowledge of God's Word as more than an end in itself. It was a means to worshipful obedience. With each thanksgiving for the truth and depths of God's Word comes another reflection on the great God who has given it for our hope, obedience, walk, and salvation.

In reference to the second verse of Psalm 119, Spurgeon says that, "those who keep the Lord's testimonies are sure to seek after himself. If this word is precious we may be sure that he himself is still more so. Personal dealing with a personal God is the longing of all those who have allowed the word of the Lord to have its full effect upon them. If we once really know the power of the gospel, we must seek the God of the gospel."[20] Spurgeon can say this because he, like the Psalmist, had been led to a deep and abiding love for God's Word. Yet, he had not found himself content with the knowledge of God's truth but pursued knowledge of the God to whom the truth pointed.

True orthodoxy should lead us to mission and worship. Although Brian McLaren has proposed a "generous orthodoxy,"[21] he ends up abandoning orthodoxy altogether. That is not the necessary reaction. Sin and pride can, and often have, polluted the pursuit of true and accurate knowledge of God in this young

---

[20] C.H. Spurgeon, *The Treasury of David*, (Peabody, Mass.: Hendrickson Publishers, 1990), 142.

[21] Brian McLaren, *A Generous Orthodoxy*, (Grand Rapids, Mich.: Zondervan, 2006).

and reformed movement. Instead of throwing out orthodoxy, we need to place it in its proper place.

Have you ever been in a place where there were no driving lanes or road signs? Without the driving lanes on the highway, there is mass confusion. People are constantly swerving in and out of danger as timid drivers share the road with reckless drivers. Add the absence of driving lanes to a highway that has no road signs, and the situation gets even worse. Now you have a road full of people unsure of how to get to their destination without any lanes to keep them traveling safely until they find their way. Orthodoxy sets the lanes and road signs on the road of the Christian journey. True doctrine lays down the boundaries and directs us to our destination so that we may travel the road safely, without spilling into oncoming traffic. Orthodoxy is not the destination, nor is it the journey itself; it is the markers and signs pointing to a greater place.

Spurgeon put it this way: "What is doctrine after all but the throne whereon Christ sitteth, and when the throne is vacant, what is the throne to us? Doctrines are the shovel and tongs of the altar, while Christ is the sacrifice smoking thereon. Doctrines are Christ's garments; verily they smell of myrrh, and cassia, and aloes out of the ivory palaces, whereby they make us glad, but it is not the garments we care for as much as the person, the very person of our Lord Jesus Christ."[22]

In the case of finding our justification in our orthodoxy, part of the problem, our desire for justification, is really at the heart of the solution. Jesus Christ is our justification; He has done this work on our behalf because we are unable to justify ourselves. Why would we settle for a hollow self-justification when the King has given up His life so that we might live?

---

[22] Iain Murray, *Spurgeon v. Hyper-Calvinism: The Battle for Gospel Preaching*, (Edinburgh: Banner of Truth Trust, 1995), 122.

If we are going to be thoroughly reformed, then we must affirm, with our forbearers, "Therefore, for any to assert that Christ is not sufficient, but that something more is required besides Him, would be too gross a blasphemy; for hence it would follow that Christ was but half a Savior."[23] Is Christ sufficient, or must it be Christ plus your preferred understanding of irresistible grace? Is Christ sufficient, or must it be accompanied by your view on the atonement?

How can we escape the pitfall of finding our justification in our orthodoxy? **By trusting in the object of our theology, Jesus, and not the accuracy of our theology.**

As a movement, we cannot, and we shall not, elevate the doctrines of grace above the Giver of Grace.

IN BRIEF

Orthodoxy, sound doctrine, is not an end in itself but is a road sign pointing to Jesus. When we attempt to root what makes us right with God (our justification) in the accuracy of what we know about God (our orthodoxy), we are bound for an endless journey in attempting to justify ourselves before God. We follow Christ who was the perfect picture of orthodoxy. He possessed perfect knowledge of God Himself, which led to worship, obedience, and humble sacrifice.

RECOMMENDED READING

Ray Ortlund's article "Justification versus Self-Justification"
A.W. Tozer's *Knowledge of the Holy*
The Belgic Confession
Ian Murray's *The Forgotten Spurgeon*
Ian Murray's *Spurgeon Versus Hyper Calvinism: The Battle for Gospel Preaching*

---

[23] *Joel Beeke, The Three Forms of Unity: Heidelberg Catechism, Belgic Confession, Canons of Dort*, (Birmingham, AL: Solid Ground Christian Books, 2010), 39.

Fleeing from the Affections

2

Have you ever heard someone say, "Take off the rose colored glasses!" When someone says this, they are implying that a person is viewing a situation with a particularly positive outlook. The assumption is that a person can remove their personality, emotions, and passions from the equation in an effort to better understand a problem or situation. So, should we take the glasses off? The logical positivists seem to think so, but with a nickname as exciting as "logical positivists," should we begin to listen to them?

Logical positivism (early 20th century) was an intellectual movement birthed in the midst of the modern period. Its leaders challenged every claim of truth to the laws of empiricism. This meant that anything that could not be tested, proven, observed, and controlled could not be said to be true. This quest has proven to be problematic; humanity has consistently demonstrated that their quest for the *pure facts*, those devoid of emotions and affections, leaves man empty and hollow. In his excellent book *Personal Knowledge*, Michael Polanyi demonstrates that every scientist personally participates in his knowledge—both its discovery and its validation. Polanyi argues that this personal involvement in the quest for knowledge is present in every pursuit of truth. This means we can never separate ourselves from the passions, emotions, and affections surrounding our personal pursuit of true knowledge.[1]

The young and reformed must be cautious that they do not make the mistake of those who would have us remove the passions, affections, and desire from the pursuit of knowledge. **To flee from the affections is not to know truth more absolutely, but to absolutely miss the point of knowing truth.**

When the heart's primary goal is to win arguments, as opposed to seeking truth, you can end up with a knowledge that is devoid of passion and persuasion. The logical positivists not only believed they could shake off the affections, but thought it necessary in order to properly seek knowledge. This same poison can find its way into the hearts and minds of the young and reformed. We can become so centered on understanding it all, that we are not struck with awe or wonder.

When I read Romans 9-11, my heart swells as Paul exalts the sovereignty of God; my mind is humbled, and on my best day, I sing along with Paul, "Oh, the depth of the riches and wisdom and knowledge of God!" (Rom. 11:33). As my father has often told me, "Good theology will lead to good doxology." The more we hold our lives up to biblical truth, the more the sheer beauty of God's grace should strike at our hearts.

As we read God's Word, we must have *selah* moments. *Selah* is a Hebrew word denoting a pause or momentary reflection on what has just been spoken or read. We find these *selah* moments throughout the Psalms, and they remind us that when we hear the words of God in the Bible, we must pause to take it all in. Like standing on a mountainside and gazing out across a wide valley, we must close our eyes and breathe in the beauty, for it is too much for just one sense to absorb. When relegated to the mind, truth becomes information accumulation, but when truth

---

[1] Michael Polanyi, *Personal Knowledge: Towards a Post-Critical Philosophy.* (Corrected ed. Chicago: University of Chicago Press, 1962).

drops from our head to our heart and hands, it becomes worship and mission!

This is why the young and reformed must read poetry; they must read the Bible and hear the tears, the dancing, the laughter, and not just the 5 notes of TULIP. It is also why we must learn from one of the great men who blended religious affections and a firm commitment to biblical truth: Jonathan Edwards. If we see the pursuit of truth as merely the collection of information, we fall short of the magnificent vision of experiencing the truth we see throughout the Bible.

Religious Affections

Religious affections are those emotions, passions, hopes, and desires that are stirred up by the Holy Spirit in the heart of those who encounter the truth of Christ. They are seen most notably in the fruits of the Spirit but are also heard in the stories, hymns, cries, and spiritual songs that fill the pages of Scripture. Although God inspires the biblical authors to write absolute truth, this absolute truth is not devoid of affection. Instead, it is full of passion and glory. Any truth that does not stir up affections leading to a holy reflection of God's glory is not worthy to be called truth. When Lloyd-Jones was describing the task of the preacher, he said, "Preaching is theology coming through a man who is on fire."[2]

There are portions of the Bible that are perpetually debated among Christians. Many of these sections are found in the writings of the Apostle Paul, and we can agree with Peter, who said, "There are some things in [Paul's letters] that are hard to understand, which the ignorant and unstable twist to their own destruction as they do the other Scriptures" (2 Peter 3:16).

[2] David Jones, *Preaching and Preachers*, (Grand Rapids, Mich.: Zondervan, 2011), 110.

One section of Paul's writings that appears to always be in the midst of the debate is chapters 9 through 11 of his letter to the Romans. Often seen as Paul's most detailed work concerning the redemptive acts of God throughout history, we must not forget that Paul was writing a letter to encourage the Christians in Rome. As he preaches and explains the work of God on behalf of the Church, his tone throughout the letter is full of conviction, passion, and worship.

Romans 9-11 is often brought into discussions about God's sovereignty—His power over salvation—and the work of election. What is often missed when discussing these passages is how Paul worships and applies the truth he is preaching to the church in Rome.

He begins by speaking of his passion to reach the lost around him, saying, "For I could wish that I myself were accursed and cut off from Christ for the sake of my brothers, my kinsmen according to the flesh" (Rom. 9:3). Before Paul even begins to dive into what is seen as the "heavy" stuff of Romans 9, he proclaims his radical commitment to reach the lost with the message of the Gospel.

After this, Paul says, "It is not as though the word of God has failed. For not all who are descended from Israel belong to Israel...Jacob I loved, but Esau I hated...so then he has mercy on whomever he wills, and he hardens whomever he wills..." (Rom. 9:6-18). These verses are often read in isolation, absent of Paul's passion, and are mistakenly assumed to be truths devoid of evangelistic fervor and urgency. In light of how Paul begins the chapter, we can almost hear his voice cracking as he lifts up the sovereignty of God in speech.

From the firm foundation of God's sovereignty in salvation, Paul then moves into Romans 10 by writing, "Brothers, my heart's desire and prayer to God for them is that they may be saved" (Rom. 10:1). Then he proclaims the truth of Romans 10:14-15,

"How then will they call on him in whom they have not believed? And how are they to believe in him of whom they have never heard? And how are they to hear without someone preaching? And how are they to preach unless they are sent? As it is written, 'How beautiful are the feet of those who preach the good news!'"

Paul is **moved** by the deep truth that God is sovereign over salvation. Paul is *affected* by the truth of who God is; that is what is meant by "religious affections." **Religious affections are the ripples in the human heart emerging from the impact that biblical truth has upon our lives.**

Paul does not stop at having his actions motivated by this deep truth. By the time he reaches the end of chapter 11, he is singing. Paul sings in Romans 11, "Oh, the depth of the riches and wisdom and knowledge of God! How unsearchable are his judgments and how inscrutable his ways! For from him and through him and to him are all things. To him be glory forever. Amen" (Rom. 11:33, 36).

The young and reformed have professed a deep commitment to the inspiration and authority of Scripture. Praise Christ that there is a renewed interest in committing all of life to the authority of God's Word. In the midst of professing this commitment to the inspiration and truth of God's Word, we must not forget to live out this profession by being shaped and molded by God's Word. Who we are, who we are becoming, our personality, and our affections, should be shaped by this God-inspired truth. When we begin to see our Bible study, the sermons we listen to, the books we read, and the conferences we attend as an opportunity to primarily learn new insider language, trendy bits of debate, or new ideas, we miss out on the great joy of being affected by the beautiful truth we so passionately profess to be intent upon knowing.

Are you affected when you hear, see, or read of who God is and what He has done? For example, does the truth of God's sovereignty over salvation lead you to mission and worship? How is your heart affected by meditating on the truth of God's Word? Jonathan Edwards said, "If the great things of religion are rightly understood, they will affect the heart."[3]

The Life of Jonathan Edwards

Jonathan Edwards is seen as one of the greatest thinkers that America has ever produced. He was a faithful pastor, prolific author, and a brilliant theologian. Edwards was born in 1703 in the American colony of Connecticut. His life included playing a part in the Great Awakening that swept across the American colonies around 1740. It was in response to reactions created by the Great Awakening that Edwards wrote what would become one of his most popular works, *The Religious Affections.*

Religious Affections was written as Edwards looked back across the Great Awakening. He was attempting to help Christians discern what were true religious affections. He wanted to know what signs accompanied the Spirit of God being at work in the midst of His people. Two camps had taken extreme sides regarding the emotional and affectionate work of God in the life of the Church. The "Old Lights," led by Charles Chauncy, had argued that reason took priority over the affections, which robbed the Christian faith of what Edwards (and the Bible) see as a great part of true belief. The "New Lights" were a group of professing Christians who believed that faith was primarily about the personal experience of God. The New Lights were led astray by all manner of religious experience, much of which was manipulated emotion and self-exaltation.

What Edwards called "religious affections" is summarized when he says, "that religion which God requires, and will

[3] Edwards, J. (1996). *A Treatise Concerning Religious Affections: In Three Parts ...* Oak Harbor, WA: Logos Research Systems, Inc.

accept, does not consist in weak, dull, and lifeless wishes, raising us but a little above a state of indifference: God, in his word, greatly insists upon it, that we be good in earnest, 'fervent in spirit,' and our hearts vigorously engaged in religion: Rom. 12:11, 'Be ye fervent in spirit, serving the Lord.' Deut. 10:12, 'And now, Israel, what doth the Lord thy God require of thee, but to fear the Lord the God, to walk in all his ways, and to love him, and to serve the Lord thy God with all thy heart, and with all thy soul?'"[4]

Edwards is pointing to passages like Deuteronomy 6:4-6 and arguing that to have religious affections means that we love God with our whole person. He wants us to join him in being caught up in the wonderful persons and works of God. Edwards wants us to join him in true religion because, "True religion is evermore a powerful thing; and the power of it appears, in the first place in the inward exercises of it in the heart, where is the principal and original seat of it."[5] Does your faith feel powerful? Does your heart rest confidently in the person and work of Jesus on your behalf?

Edwards stood in the middle of these two camps and argued that, "As in worldly things, worldly affections are very much the spring of men's motion and action; so in religious matters, the spring of their actions is very much religious affection: he that has doctrinal knowledge and speculation only, without affection, never is engaged in the business of religion."[6]

Edwards was never satisfied with the two extremes of denying or abusing the role that affection, emotion, and passion

[4] Edwards, J. (1996). *A Treatise Concerning Religious Affections: In Three Parts ...* Oak Harbor, WA: Logos Research Systems, Inc.

[5] Edwards, J. (1996). *A Treatise Concerning Religious Affections: In Three Parts ...* Oak Harbor, WA: Logos Research Systems, Inc.

[6] Edwards, J. (1996). *A Treatise Concerning Religious Affections: In Three Parts ...* Oak Harbor, WA: Logos Research Systems, Inc.

play in Christian worship. Instead, he cast a vision that holds unswervingly to the sure foundation of Christian doctrine while at the same time acknowledging the affections and passion that true belief and faith stirs up in the human heart.

This is important because true religious affections spring out of a heart that desires intimacy with Christ. These religious affections stir us up to radical faith, worship, mission, and obedience. Edwards claimed, "Such is man's nature, that he is very inactive, any otherwise than he is influenced by some affection, either love or hatred, desire, hope, fear, or some other. These affections we see to be the springs that set men going, in all the affairs of life, and engage them in all their pursuits: these are the things that put men forward, and carry them along, in all their worldly business; and especially are men excited and animated by these, in all affairs wherein they are earnestly engaged, and which they pursue with vigor."[7]

The will rests in the affections—the heart. If the heart remains unmoved, then the actions (the will) will never move. This claim strikes right at the heart of the difference between works based religion and the Gospel. Works based religion seeks to transform the actions in an effort to see the heart change, which leads to a life of hollow obedience that rarely lasts. The Gospel addresses the heart, knowing that if the heart is moved by the grace of God, the will (actions) will emerge as fruit of God's gracious work.

The affections are where the power to kill sin comes from. The affections are where evangelistic urgency comes from. The desire to speak and listen to God in prayer and Bible study emerges from these religious affections. The fruits of the Spirit are the manifestation of these religious affections in the life of the believer.

---

[7] Edwards, J. (1996). *A Treatise Concerning Religious Affections: In Three Parts ...* Oak Harbor, WA: Logos Research Systems, Inc.

Edwards' life was full of meditation on the wonders of God. He would take long walks while writing in his journal and contemplating the wonders of God seen in the Bible, nature, and human relationships. As he meditated on the beauties of God throughout the world, his heart was stirred up to a deep worship and piety. Edwards would ask, "Is there anything which Christians can find in heaven or earth, so worthy to be the objects of their admiration and love, their earnest and longing desires, their hope, and their rejoicing, and their fervent zeal, as those things that are held forth to us in the gospel of Jesus Christ?"[8]

The young and reformed must be cautious that the truths of God are not merely knowledge that remains in our heads, never dropping to our hearts and hands. The Bible does not conceive of knowing God in a way that does not lead to genuine worship, mission, and obedience. We should be caught up in meditating and reflecting on God through our study of Scripture, our prayer life, and the books we read. Anything that does not leave us craving more of Christ should be put on the shelf for that which fills us with desire for the beauty of our Lord.

We must be aware that the affections, passions, emotions, hopes, and desires of the heart should be molded by sound biblical doctrine. Knowing that we cannot trust all the spirits (1 John 4), we must test our attitudes, affections, and spirits. Any of the affections that do not lift up Christ must be discarded as selfish pursuits. While we must be cautious that we are not caught up in fleeting emotions, we must also never abandon the beauty and importance that holy affections and passions play in the Christian life. Affections and passions are rooted in biblical truth, not detached from it.

---

[8] Edwards, J. (1996). *A Treatise Concerning Religious Affections: In Three Parts ...* Oak Harbor, WA: Logos Research Systems, Inc.

Charles Spurgeon found that there are some who "could write a treatise upon anything in the Bible, and a great many things besides...who like to hear true doctrine; but it never penetrates their inner man."[9] The young and reformed must be careful that we don't stumble into becoming like those who could write an essay about God, but do not desire Him with our affections. Are you caught up in the beautiful truth of who God is and what He has done? Does God captivate your heart? Do the works of God steal your thoughts?

A Dull Knowledge

Take time to remember the most boring teacher you ever had. When did you have that teacher? What was the subject? I can remember a teacher that drove me to the edge of my sanity; we will call him Dr. Bruce.

Dr. Bruce was an absolutely brilliant biologist, but he was not passionate about his subject. He had grown bored with the wonder that had attracted him to studying this particular facet of God's creation. The genetic code that had once glued him to his microscope now came across in his lectures as old news. Since Dr. Bruce seemed to hate Biology, I hated Biology.

When knowledge sits still in our mind, never bursting from our heart and hands, we can grow bored with even the most profound truth. As we work to understand God and the world He has created for His glory and our joy, we must see that "to treat any subject without reference to God's glory is not scholarship, but insurrection."[10] When we treat each subject as an opportunity to see the glory of God on display, we are

---

[9] Charles Spurgeon, *Spurgeon's Sermons Volume One*, (Peabody: Hendrickson, 2011), 95.

[10] John Piper, *The Pleasures of God: Meditations on God's Delight in Being God*. (Rev. and expanded ed. Sisters, Or: Multnomah Publishers, 2000), 298.

working to unite the religious affections with the pursuit of truth.

Are you bored with a perversion of Christianity that is merely intellectually hobby? I sure am!

In John Piper's excellent book, *The Pleasures of God*, he quotes Thomas Goodwin, saying, "Indeed, thoughts and affections are the mutual causes of each other: 'While I meditated, the fire burned;' so that thoughts are the bellows that kindle and inflame affections; and then if they are inflamed, they cause thoughts to boil; therefore men newly converted to God, having new and strong affections, can with more pleasure think of God than any."[11] The glory that saturates all of life under the Lordship of Christ captivates the human heart and leaves it longing for more. This desire, this longing, leads us to humbly pursue truth and glory in all things.

It is neither beneficial nor possible to have a passionless view of truth. Although some may claim that they have an unbiased view of truth, they have merely substituted passion for God's glory with passion for their own self-worship. They may despise the idea of God's standards affecting how you learn and study, but they are focused on how their standards are violated or affirmed in the pursuit of truth.

What is your passion? What are you affected by? What do you spend your time dreaming about? Your daydreams and ambitions will tell a vivid story about who you are and what you worship. Aristotle suggested that everything moves to its own good. What is the good that you move towards? If you are motivated by your own self-advancement, then you will be affected by the way the world defines success. If you are motivated by the growth of a cause (however noble the cause may be), then you will be affected by how many people rally

[11] Quoted in John Piper, *The Pleasures of God: Meditations on God's Delight in Being God.* (Rev. and expanded ed. Sisters, Or: Multnomah Publishers, 2000), 296.

around your cause. But if you are motivated by the glory of God, then every cause, pursuit, and ambition will be affected by that glory. This will produce religious affections.

The quest to seek truth, beauty, love, and goodness will be affected. The quest for the good life does not happen in a vacuum, so what will your pursuit of truth be influenced by? I urge you, along with the Bible and Jonathan Edwards, to know God and to make Him known through the influence of holy religious affections.

Affectionate Theology

Have you ever listened to blues? I'm not talking about the cover band down the street...I'm talking about Son House, Buddy Guy, Muddy Waters type of blues. Great blues draws you deeper into the music the longer you listen to a specific piece. At the beginning of Robert Johnson's "Preachin' Blues," you are a different person then you are by the end, because blues music *affects* the listener. Many dismiss blues because of its simplicity, but when you just sit and listen to where a talented blues musician takes you, you will find yourself in a different place then where you began. The blues singer sings from a place of deep affection to impact the listener. In a similar fashion, a preacher in tune with genuine religious affections preaches to "make an impression on the heart on the spot."[12]

Edwards could have seen the abuses of the Great Awakening and gone on to dismiss the precious beauty found in the religious affections. He could have seen that the complexity of human brokenness would always create the opposite dangers of being too focused on experiencing God or too indifferent to feeling His presence. Yet, the glory of Christ is too rich to be

---

[12] David Jones, *Preaching and Preachers*, (Grand Rapids, Mich.: Zondervan, 2011), 94.

relegated to merely the mind's thoughts. The heart and hands hunger to know God deeply and to make Him known widely.

As the world grows apathetic to reflection and careless with its emotions, Christians have the unique privilege of being people who worship "in spirit" and "in truth" (John 4:24). Never content to leave us with a one-dimensional picture of life, the Bible paints a glorious picture of the role of the affections and passions in knowing God and making Him known throughout the world.

The young and reformed must be careful not to miss the beauty and wonder of this Christ exalting truth. What joy it is to have the deep truth of who God is and what He has done to inform our minds *and* pierce our hearts! Sure, we have seen the abuses of feel-good Christianity. We have seen the anti-intellectualism of our respective denominations. We have seen the sappy cotton candy karaoke that passes for worship. The answer to these failures is not to abandon the role that godly affections and emotions play in the Christian life, but to place these affections on the foundation of biblical truth.

So, how do we practice an affectionate theology?

It starts with realizing that the heart and the mind are not divided. Truth and affection are not at odds. Biblical, Christ-centered, gospel-saturated truth will lead to deep affections! A lie has seeped into the life of the Church that argues for the separation between fact and value. We think that what we believe and how we live can be separated quite easily by realizing that facts and values (our passions, convictions, and affections) have no real relationship at all. This lie is a poison bent upon hollowing out any significance in the Christian faith. The Word of God is clear that we are to love God with "all [our] heart and with all [our] soul and with all [our] might" (Deut. 6:5). There is no division between bold truth and deep affections in the life of the Christians!

We then intentionally begin asking of all of our knowledge, "So what?" We dare not reduce our faith to a series of intellectual assents to propositions. God is just. So, what does the glorious truth of God's justice lead me to? Does it lead me to see His justice exacted upon Christ for my sins? Does it lead me to live a life of justice? Lloyd-Jones reminds us, "You and I can be absolutely right and orthodox in doctrine and yet wrong in spirit."[13]

Does your knowledge of God help you walk with the Holy Spirit? It is only when we are in step with the Spirit that true religious affections will well up in our lives. **We are not called to be wrapped up in emotionalism, but to have our emotions stirred as we meditate on the truth of God's Word.** Again, Lloyd-Jones is particularly insightful when he points out that, "Emotionalism is a state and a condition in which the emotions have run riot. The emotions are in control...the emotions are to be approached through the understanding, through the mind, by truth."[14]

Finally, we trust in our sovereign God. Proverbs 3:5-6 brings warmth to my soul when I hear it say, "Trust in the Lord with all your heart, and do not lean on your own understanding. In all your ways acknowledge him, and he will make straight your paths." We can be confident that if our desire is to honor the Lord, He will constantly be examining our heart by His Word. Our desires and affections will be in submission to His precepts, and we can pursue true religious affections. We can come before our sovereign God and ask that He would "save us from being so afraid of the false that we quench the Spirit of God, and become respectable, and so pseudo-intellectual that the Spirit of God is kept back, and we go on in our dryness and aridity, and in our comparative futility, and helplessness, and uselessness."[15]

---

[13] David Jones, *Revival*, (Westchester, Ill.: Crossway Books, 1987), 64.

[14] Ibid; 75.

[15] Ibid; 79.

If we humbly come before the Lord, begging him to lead us to genuine affections, asking to know the power of His presence, He will lead us.

We must exchange the sappy for the substantial. Do away with a convenient Christianity in order to pursue the comfort of the gospel. We must resist letting emotions dictate the truth, so that they can glory in the truth. Let us cast out hollow happiness and replace it with genuine joy. Let the thoughts of our mind sing the harmony to the melody in our hearts as we live out the song of Christ through the rhythm of our hands.

IN BRIEF

Christians are not called to be people driven by their emotions, but we must not drive out the emotions either. God has called us to "taste and see that the Lord is good!" (Ps. 34:8). Why would we settle for relegating the beauty and richness of who God is and what He has done to merely one aspect of our experience?

FURTHER READING

Religious Affections by Jonathan Edwards
The Pleasures of God by John Piper
Revival by DM Lloyd-Jones
Valley of Vision by Arthur Bennet
Joy of Calvinism by Greg Forster

A "Runaway" Reformation

3

Have you ever seen a guillotine—the machine that was used during the French Revolution to behead nobles like Marie Antoinette?

The guillotine might serve as the symbol for the French Revolution (1789-1799) and, more specifically, the "Reign of Terror," which lasted for about a year. During this time thousands of political nobles were killed after the people overthrew the French government.

The guillotine is not just an appropriate symbol for the French Revolution but for general revolution as well. A revolution has at its core the desire to cut off from the status quo in order to establish a new order or idea. Revolutions and revolutionaries are reactionary. They sever ties with the current way of doing things, usually in an abrupt and violent way.

Therefore, revolution is *not* synonymous with reformation.

Genuine reformation requires men and women to remain faithful in their churches as they exercise God-glorifying stewardship over the people and resources God has placed in their care. The young and reformed movement must be willing to express a holy patience with churches that have been faithful to God, the gospel, and missions while actively praying and humbly lifting up the Word of God as the centerpiece for all doctrine, worship, and practice.

The Reformation and French Revolution both produced results that have altered history, but they went about achieving those results in vastly different ways. The Reformation leaders embraced the truth that all men are broken in their sin apart from Christ, and the solution is not a transfer of power from one party to the next but a humble submission to the sovereign God. The leaders of the French Revolution held the belief that man was the measure of all truth and goodness and that a collective grouping of those not in power could displace the corrupt in power and create a utopian society by their own will and knowledge.

Reformed theology did not emerge in the ivory tower of the university. Nor did it emerge in the desert caves of the Gnostics. Rather, it emerged in the hearts and minds of pastors and priests across Europe who were willing to endure excommunication, exile, and death to see the people of God in their churches, local communities, and nations submit their lives to the deep truths of God's Word.

Join with the long line of men and women who waited for years, sometimes in suffering, for God's people to see the depths of God's Word. How long did Calvin labor diligently in Geneva? How faithful was Edwards in Northampton? How long did Carey wait to see his first convert in India?

There is a heritage of godly men and women who fill our bookshelves—brothers and sisters who waited patiently for the Lord to move in the heart of His church. Don't abandon your local church because they are slow to change. You must persevere and allow your life to speak of the beautiful sovereign grace you so adore.

We must carefully examine the concept of reformation, the biblical model for change, the example of Luther, and how a "runaway" reformation abandons the mission of God in the local church.

A God-Centered, Church-Changing Reformation

At the beginning, many young movements desire to abandon any current institutions and organizations that either disagree or fall short of the standards of the new movement.

The Protestant Reformation has largely been seen as the great exodus of those who had things *right* from those who were unwilling to change. We forget that when Luther wrote and nailed *The Ninety-Five Theses,* he was acting as an agent of reformation inside the Catholic religious system. It wasn't until they were trying to excommunicate and kill him that he jumped off the Papal ship. Though his thoughts, ideas, and writings were flying in the face of the Catholic status quo, he genuinely believed he could help be an agent of change in calling the Catholic Church to repentance.

Reformation is something that happens within a system, not by fleeing the system, even if it is plagued with problems. At the heart of the reformation, and reformed theology, is the desire to see one's brothers and sisters come to a deeper relationship with the Triune God and a deeper affection for His glory and exaltation. **Genuine change cannot occur if we persistently run from the tension and struggle present in our local churches and denominations.**

In these days of what has been called "post-denominationalism," it is in vogue to escape the captivity of one's familiar or traditional theological traditions and flee to a more *suitable* location for one to conduct both life and theology. This has been seen across the board as it has been clear that many young reformed individuals are attempting to jump out of their historic mainline evangelical denominations (Catholic, Baptist, Presbyterian, Methodist) and jump into other protestant denominations. I have seen many men from my particular tradition (Baptist) become frustrated with the slow work of leading others into the depths of reformed theology. They assume that jumping into another tradition will resolve their theological conflicts.

Many men and women have also abandoned their historic mainline denominations in frustration with the slow nature of change within these traditions. They opt to move into churches that are not connected with historic traditions. These churches become independent or non-denominational bodies in an effort to distance themselves from the abuses, problems, or growing pains of many historic expressions of the Christian faith. We must be cautious and gentle in our estimation of these churches, many of which emerge from pure hearts set on the glory and mission of God. We must be cautious that we don't abandon our denominations and traditions merely because they don't keep up with the pace of change we desire them to maintain.

I am by no means discounting those who the Spirit of God leads to move from one tradition to the next. I do believe that sometimes the Lord calls people to a new denominational home. Surely, if a person comes to a place in their reading of scripture where their theological beliefs have differed in a way that would put their convictions in affirming the beliefs of their church in jeopardy, they may need to relocate to another Christian church. There is a place for God moving men and women into denominations that are more in line with their convictions and outside of denominations that may restrain the work of the Lord; my concern is directed towards the youthful impatience this movement is in danger of encouraging.

Even so, the greater danger—one many local churches have already felt the brunt of—is that some young and reformed men and women run into local churches demanding quick doctrinal or philosophical changes without respect to the current state of the church. When the necessary changes (usually involving theological minutiae) aren't made in the manner or with the speed expected by these impatient "reformers," they flee in an attempt to find a church that better suits their theological appetites.

Men and women who have been influenced by the young and reformed movement can bring energy and enthusiasm into local churches that need the revitalization that comes with a renewed emphasis on the Word of God and the work of God in salvation. But if these wonderful truths are not communicated in a spirit of humility, they can destroy local churches already suffering from pride, division, and biblical naïveté.

When those among the young and reformed flee churches that will not adjust to their "convictions," they bring their baggage, preferences, and discontentment with them. Sometimes they go and start a new work so they can point the finger at the watered down churches around the block. They do this in the name of reformation, yet what ends up happening is that these groups begin to devalue the work of God through other Christian communities that don't line up with their theology. Wilson sees this for what it is when he observes that, "by calling for immediate reformation now in a loud voice, they mask their refusal to reform themselves. In the work of reformation, they make haste, but not slowly."[1]

The perseverance of this generation has yet to be tested. We have grown up in a world where change is expected to happen quickly and efficiently, but churches do not abide by these "rules" of speed and return on investment. There are many young men going into the pulpits are entering with a naïveté that leads them to assume that they should expect to see change happen quickly and visibly. They assume that they should be held in the same regard that Edwards or Calvin were held among their congregations, not realizing that those men suffered for decades at the hands of the people God had placed under their stewardship as they attempted to lead their people well.

---

[1] Douglas Wilson, *Mother Kirk: Essays and Forays in Practical Ecclesiology,* (Moscow, Idaho: Canon Press, 2001), 83.

The Biblical Model for Change

The Reformation creed of *semper reformanda*, "always reforming," is concerned with a lifelong willingness to change our lives, doctrine, and worship as we encounter the light of God's Word.

So what does the Bible say about change?

First, the Bible does not see change as negative. When we look at the Bible, we see a vision for change that is Godward, healing, and communal. When God placed Adam and Eve in the garden, He gave them the "cultural mandate" to, "be fruitful, multiply and subdue" (Gen. 1:26-30). In a meaningful way, cultivation is ingrained into the image of God and is expressed through our humanity. God created us as agents of cultivation. The ability to affect change is a gift given for worship unto God.

After sin entered the world, cultivating and subduing creation was broken and made difficult by sin. God says, "cursed is the ground because of you; in pain you shall eat of it all the days of your life; thorns and thistles it shall bring forth for you; and you shall eat the plants of the field. By the sweat of your face..." (Gen. 3:17-19). Although the Bible casts a vision for cultivation and change, the entrance of sin has put this process on a hard and difficult path. God created us as agents of cultivation, the fall fractured this responsibility, and in Christ we are now agents of restoration.

Change is going to be slow and difficult because it requires sacrifice and perseverance from those who desire to be agents of change.

In the prophets we see this painful labor for restoration. When we look at the prophetic voice throughout God's Word, we see men who were genuine reformers. These prophets were not innovators or revolutionaries, they were people called by God to challenge the wandering hearts of God's people. Michael

Williams points out that, "the prophets denounce not the institutions of Hebrew religion but rather what the Israelites had come to make of these things."[2] When we hear the voice of God crying out through Amos that He "cannot stand your assemblies. Even though you bring me burnt offerings and grain offerings, I will not accept them" (Amos. 5:21-22), we hear the voice of God working through an agent of reform to call Israel back to the covenant.

The prophetic voice must be the paradigm for the way the young and reformed approach their role as agents of reformation in the context of the local church. Do you know what all of the prophets of the Bible experienced before they began to cry for change? God brought them to a place of brokenness and humility, usually in a painful way.

Jonah was swallowed by the whale. Isaiah was brought into the awful holiness of the Lord. Hosea was wed to a whore. Jeremiah endured endless persecution. And John the Baptist was called into an extremely uncomfortable lifestyle only to be beheaded for the truth.

None of these men were revolutionaries. They were reformers. They didn't suffer for creating new ideas or new religions; they suffered for pointing back to Yahweh God. Michael Williams lends his voice to the idea of the prophets as reformers when he reminds us that the Old Testament prophetic message, "[did] not entail a rejection or even a revision of the Mosaic revelation. Quite the contrary: the prophets, as reformers, seek to call Israel back to the covenant's original meaning and vitality."[3]

The restoration the prophets sought was not detached from God's people. Instead, it was focused on the people of God. We

---

[2] Michael Williams, *Far As the Curse is Found: The Covenant Story of Redemption.* (Phillipsburg, NJ: P & R Pub., 2005), 190.

[3] Ibid.

often speak of reform and restoration on such a large level that we miss out on the spheres where we can actually affect this restoration and change: local churches and local communities. Habakkuk was not primarily burdened for the people of Israel; he was burdened for the people of Judah. Why? Because they were his people.

In Luke 19:41, Jesus approaches the city of Jerusalem, and it is said, "he wept over it." He did not weep for the people in Laodicea; John would weep for them. He did not weep for the people in Corinth; Paul would weep for them. I do not weep for the people in New York; but my brothers and sisters in NYC do. I weep for those in Southeast Texas and Dallas-Fort Worth. The people in these areas are the people God has yoked my heart and soul to, and one day this might change, but my desire to see faithful reform and restoration is committed to the people in these cities and the churches pursuing Christ there.

If the young and reformed are genuinely interested in seeing change come to Christianity in the West, they must bring their grand vision to their local churches with a faithful heart. They must seek restoration that pushes the people of God further into the worship and mission of the person of God.

Let us have a grand vision for what God can do in our cities, nations, and world—but let us also allow this grand vision pull us deeper into our local churches and communities.

The Example of Luther

As the hammer nailed the piece of paper against the large door at the Castle Church in Wittenberg, Luther stood confident that if the Roman Catholic Church listened to his criticisms, true reform might happen.

Martin Luther was a deeply introspective Augustinian monk who was sent off to study theology by his mentor so that he would stop fixating on his tortured heart and soul. As Luther began to study the work of Augustine, he was drawn into the writings of the Apostle Paul, and he made a shocking discovery: he was sinful and God demanded a righteousness that Luther himself could not provide. For a man already prone to despair, this revelation shook Luther to his core. It appears that a deep study of Romans 1 led Luther to reevaluate God and salvation. In the process he realized that Paul did not stop in Romans 1 but went on to say, "but God shows his love for us in that while we were still sinners, Christ died for us. Since, therefore, we have now been justified by his blood, much more shall we be saved by him from the wrath of God" (Rom. 5:8-9).

The truth that God's righteous requirements have been met on our behalf in Jesus led Luther to a deep reflection and focus on the doctrine of justification by faith alone. The doctrine of justification by faith alone reminds us that sinful humans are justified (made right before God) by faith in Jesus Christ and His finished work. As Luther dug into the Word of God and realized the truth that justification by faith alone was the foundation of salvation, he began to look around at the Catholic Church. He realized that many of their practices were completely contrary to the word of God concerning salvation. Most offensive to Luther was the selling of indulgences. Indulgences were pardons for sin, and the Catholic Church was funding their extravagant building projects in Rome by selling indulgences that would free people from the punishment for their sins.

When Luther realized how ridiculous the idea of indulgences was in light of God's Word, he drafted 95 theses that he hoped would start a debate within the church that would in turn lead church leadership to change the false practices. Luther was not a revolutionary. He was a reformer. The work of Luther helped set the stage for the protestant reformation across all of Europe. Kuyper said of Luther, "To a great extent Calvin entered upon the harvest of what the hero of Wittenberg had sown in and outside Germany."[4]

When Luther entered a debate in Leipzig, after he posted *The Ninety-Five Theses* but before the Pope excommunicated him, he was charged with following after John Hus, who had split from the Catholic Church completely in order to keep in line with his reformed convictions. Luther's response was that he had "never approved of their schism. Even though they had divine right on their side, they ought not to have withdrawn from the Church, because the highest divine right is unity and charity."[5]

Luther did not see breaking away from the church, even though they were walking in error, as the immediate reaction to encountering the truth of God's Word. Although Luther eventually left Rome, he did not do so flippantly, but was forced out for attempting to bring biblical reformation. **Luther hoped to see the Catholic Church reformed, not reinvented.**

The Failure of a "Runaway" Reformation

In *The Screwtape Letters*, C.S. Lewis insightfully demonstrates many trappings and pitfalls involved in the pursuit of God. Screwtape, a demon, writes to his nephew attempting to tempt and test a man who has been united to Christ in salvation and is now living the Christian life. He says regarding church, "Surely you know that if a man can't be cured of churchgoing, the next best thing is to send him all over the neighborhood looking for the church that 'suits' him until he becomes a taster or connoisseur of churches."[6]

---

[4] Abraham Kuyper, *Lectures on Calvinism*, (New York: Cosimo Inc., 2007), 22.

[5] Quoted in Roland Bainton, *Here I stand: a life of Martin Luther.* (Peabody, Mass.: Hendrickson Publishers, 2009), 101.

[6] C.S. Lewis, *Screwtape Letters*, (New York: HarperCollinsPublishers, 2000), 81.

A "connoisseur of churches," is one who runs all over the neighborhood looking for a church that "fits" their agenda. If this was relevant in Lewis' day, it is even more relevant in this day when the "me" culture of America has climaxed in the elevation of radical freedom of choice and the Christian person views the church as a vending machine meant to meet their needs.

It is not the primary purpose of the church to meet our needs. While the young and reformed have decided they agree with that truth in principle, in practice they have abandoned this in favor of treating the church as a platform for their newfound ideas. If we truly desire to see change in our churches, we must love our churches. If we desire to be effective in that change, then the change must point our churches back to God and not forward to a new agenda. If we desire that change to last, then we must be willing to dig into the trenches for the long haul.

I have often been asked, "When does a church become a synagogue of Satan?" In other words, "how far can a church go and still be a church that worships the God of the Bible?" When a church begins to deny those things that undermine the saving work of Christ on behalf of sinners that is when a church is no longer worshiping the God of the Bible. If a church denies the Trinity, they have stepped outside of being a Christian church. If a church denies the deity of Christ, they have stepped outside of being a Christian church. If you find yourself in a church that is abandoning core doctrines of the faith, then for the spiritual health of you and your family, you should leave.

Ironically, the very same poison that plagues the "seeker-sensitive" church movement is found among the young and reformed. The "seeker-sensitive" method thought that by losing the traditional aspects of the worship gathering they could accommodate those who were not comfortable or familiar with church environments. This movement sought to meet the desires of the worldly individual in an effort to demonstrate that the transition from apathy towards spiritual things and the Christian life was not that drastic. Those critical of this movement are shaking their heads in disagreement, and yet, I think that many among those in the young and reformed movement have allowed a different set of desires to shape the idea that church exists to meet their needs. Within the "seeker sensitive" group, the needs are primarily social and economic, but among the young and reformed, the needs become nuanced theological convictions (often only half-understood), theological labels, trendy worship services, and social dynamics.

The church exists for the worship of God through the administration of the ordinances of God (baptism and communion), the preaching of God's Word, and the fellowship of believers. When the young and reformed begin to bow down to the idol of preferences, expressed in a desire for theological purity detached from humility and love, they begin to mirror the selfishness of the world.

We must accept, as the Westminster Confession states, that "the purest churches under heaven are subject both to mixture and error; and some have so degenerated as to become no churches of Christ, but synagogues of Satan. Nevertheless, there shall be always a Church on earth to worship God according to his will."[7] If you are a part of a church that is a "synagogue of Satan,"[8] then it is healthy for you to leave and find a Christ-exalting church. But if you are a part of a church that doesn't match your definition of a pure church, remember that you contribute as much impurity

---

[7] G.I. Williamson, *The Westminster Confession of Faith for Study Classes,* (2nd ed. Phillipsburg, N.J.: P & R Pub., 2004), 247.

[8] Although the Westminster Confession was primarily addressing the Catholic institution, and using harsh words to do so, it can be said that the concern was not primarily with any one Christian tradition but with any church professing to be a Christian church that does not lift up the person and work of Christ in salvation.

as the next person. **The biggest obstacle to the work of God in restoring and reforming your church is the sin that is nestled near your heart.**

A "runaway" reformation will fail. If the young and reformed fall and remain in this pitfall of abandoning local churches and historic traditions for the flare and glitter of the cult of the "new," then we will be remembered as a movement with great potential but no perseverance. We need men and women entering churches that are humbled by the depths of Reformed theology. They must be willing to press into Christ and persevere in faithfulness to their churches as they graciously and joyfully lift up the person of Christ according to the truth of God's Word.

This push to persevere in the communities of faith in which God has placed us is going to require a gospel-driven patience. "Impatience in the ministry is a sign of a revolutionary temperament, as opposed to reformational commitment."[9] Revolutionaries and reformers are vastly different people.

Local Reformation

So should you draft an outline of all your theological positions and nail them to the front door of your local church?

I would not suggest this course of action. Remember, Luther was emerging as an agent of reformation within what the Westminster Confession might call a "synagogue of Satan." The methods were extreme because the error was extreme. Luther attempted to reform the foundations of the Catholic Church because the problems ran that deep. Accept the fact that Luther's platform is not your own, and be glad about it, for it was Luther's burden to bear.

9 Douglas Wilson, *Mother Kirk: Essays and Forays in Practical Ecclesiology,* (Moscow, Idaho: Canon Press, 2001), 82.

Ask that God would give you a broken heart over the people in your context. Your local church and community are full of people desperate for the gospel of grace. You have never met someone who did not need to hear the gospel of Jesus Christ, so don't waste your time trying to be a revolutionary; be a reformer. Don't run past the people that God has placed in your Christian community; rather, walk with them.

This is a call to pastors, elders, deacons, husbands, wives, Sunday school teachers, Bible study leaders, missional community hosts, professors, and seminary students. Let us lock arms with the people God has placed under our responsibility, even if it is but a few, and walk with them into the depths of God's grace. Don't castigate the man who denies the full sovereignty of God in salvation. Love him unconditionally, and search the scriptures with him. Don't alienate the leader with a shepherd's heart because he can't sign off on limited atonement. Gently lead him into the beauty and freedom found in the truth of the effectual salvation Christ accomplished on the cross.

Those who are not involved in vocational ministry but faithfully serve local churches should seek to be faithful in their stewardship. It is easy to identify and point the finger at the "church problems" while looking past the small issues that we could apply our energies, knowledge, and affections to help solve. Churches will have problems until the return of Jesus because they will always be made up of people. If you want to see a deeper appreciation for the doctrines of grace, I suggest you grab a handful of young men or women and begin to pour the truth of God's grace into their lives. **Rather than complain and abandon, stay and restore.** The church needs the theology that has shaken your heart to flesh out through your life and bring leadership, encouragement, and mission to the body of Christ.

How are we to act as agents of reformation in our current setting? I can't say it better than Doug Wilson: "Our approach must be patient, biblical, and inductive, and never ideological, abstract, and deductive. When a revolutionary mind gets hold of an abstract ideological system (and it does not matter whether he calls it Marxism or Calvinism) and conducts all 'reforms' in terms of deductions made from his abstraction in the sky, he has become what Hoffer pointedly called the 'true believer.'"[10] Wilson's description of our approach to reform sounds like it must grow from hearts that have put on "compassionate hearts, kindness, humility, meekness, and patience, bearing with one another and, if one has a complaint against another, forgiving each other; as the Lord has forgiven you, so you also must forgive. And above all these put on love, which binds everything together in perfect harmony" (Col. 3:12-14).

When revolutionaries enter churches, they are not carrying a cross—they are beating a drum. For the revolutionary, "the 'truth' represented by the cause no longer matters, the cause does. And people just get in the way."[11] But for reformers, the church is full of people who should be gently shepherded through the long and difficult process of shaping our lives in accordance with the light of God's Word.

Isaiah 66:2 says, "This is the one to whom I will look: he who is humble and contrite in spirit and trembles at my word." Would we be characterized as humble and contrite? Are we those who tremble at the Word of God? *The Valley of Vision* reminds us yet again of our humility before God: "O thou God of all grace, make me more thankful, more humble; Inspire me with a deep sense of my unworthiness arising from the depravity of my nature, my omitted duties, my unimproved

---

[10] Ibid; 82.

[11] Ibid.

advantages, thy commands violated by me...Then send me out to make him known to my fellow-men." [12]

May all you reformed men and women walk into your homes, local churches, Bible studies, and seminary classes with a limp. When you are absolutely broken by the power of God's grace, people will long for the restoration they see and hear in your life. In other words, lead by example.

Are you beating a drum or carrying a cross?

IN BRIEF

If we want to see genuine change brought to the church, we must be willing to persevere in faithfulness to our local congregations and historic denominations. We must lead those whom we often drag behind us. If we want to follow in the example of the reformed men and women who have influenced us, we must be willing to hold fast to the local church and walk with those in our Christian community who we may not completely agree with. We must learn to disagree and not allow our disagreement to lead to division.

FURTHER READING

Martin Luther by Roland Bainton
The Reformation: How a Monk and a Mallet Changed the World by
      Stephen Nichols
Mother Kirk by Douglas Wilson
Reformation: Yesterday, Today and Tomorrow by Carl Trueman

---

[12] Arthur Bennet, *The Valley of Vision: A collection of Puritan Prayers and Devotions*, (Edinburgh: Banner of Truth Trust, 1975), 327.

The Precious Few

4

What comes to mind when you hear the word *cult*? Grape juice? Mountaintop compounds filled with guns and rations? Men with countless wives attempting to create their own city?

When we think of cults, we generally think of groups of small-minded individuals who buy into the crazy ideas of a charismatic leader. At the core of a cult is the idea that there is something unique about the knowledge of the leader or group that separates them from "others." The "others" are everyone who has not experienced the knowledge that the cult has obtained.

Any collection of people: social clubs, organizations, causes, churches, etc., can become insulated from the outside world. When these groups insulate themselves from the world, they separate themselves. And when they separate themselves, they harden the distinctions between themselves and everyone else. This is not a new thing.

Even in the earliest days of the church, communities sprang up that claimed to have a secret knowledge. These people were referred to as "Gnostics," and their ideas flew under the banner of "Gnosticism." The name "Gnostic" came from the Greek word *gnosis*, which meant "knowledge." These cults found their identity in secret knowledge, which led to the development of a "two-tiered system of Christians...with spiritual believers being able [allegedly] to understand the mysteries of Scripture that simple believers could not appreciate."[1]

The knowledge cults of the Gnostics could be illustrated by separating people into two groups: those who "get it" and those who don't. Consider this: after months of attending a Bible study with the same group of guys, the leader begins to move the focus of study to the book of Romans. Rather than using the book of Romans to encourage the believers under his stewardship to a deeply affectionate and practical theology, he wields the letter like a knife, cutting away at those in the group who do not immediately share his opinion on the theological content of the letter. He wants the study to have a "we're all in this together" vibe, but he has clearly identified those in the group who are "in the know" while those on the margins grow increasingly more frustrated with the constant insider language and arguing.

The Reformed community is in danger of quickly becoming a group of "enlightened" persons who have found the key to understanding the "depths and riches of the wisdom and knowledge of God" (Romans 11:33). Like a high school boy pumped full of steroids, our theological culture has the appearance of knowledge, but our knowledge does not breed humility or action. Similar to the Gnostic communities that emerged in the early church, we take shelter in our sub-culture and refuse to expose ourselves to brothers and sisters who do not possess our secret knowledge.

The Internet has become our version of the desert caves, and we have agreed on a set of unspoken rules. We have resolved to read no materials other than those published by Reformed publishers. We have guardians for our community,

[1]   Gregg Allison, *Historical Theology: An Introduction to Christian Doctrine: A Companion to Wayne Grudem's Systematic Theology*, (Grand Rapids, Mich.: Zondervan, 2011), 123.

a host of our favorite "reformed" bloggers who become the gateway to any and all media that we consume. We are unflinchingly certain that prior to His ascension, Christ blessed the ESV translation. We laugh at people who try to "Fireproof" their marriage, and we think that Dave Ramsey is a "cover up" for a false health and wealth gospel (as we go into consumer debt because we have not translated our belief in the sovereignty of God into a practical discipline of money management). We speak an insider language that appeals to no one outside of our small circles, and instead of joining in on the symphony that God is creating in the church at large, we are content with being a collection of single note musicians.

Why have we done this? Is knowledge evil? Is it wrong to have theological standards or to hold those who profess to be stewards of the gospel to a biblical standard? By no means!

But when our standard becomes a brick wall instead of a filter, we lose all connection with a world filled with the lost and brothers and sisters who have arrived at different theological interpretations. When we embrace the method of the Gnostics, we slam the door in the face of the very people we are called to go and bring the good news to. The young and reformed, like the Gnostics, can start to treat themselves as the "precious few" who get it.

We need to look at what the Bible says about knowledge, consider the Word of God through the Apostle John, listen closely to Calvin, and ask ourselves which is more fundamental: to know about God or to be known by God?

The Bible and Knowledge

So what does the Bible say about knowledge? It appears that the desire for knowledge gets Adam and Eve in trouble in Genesis 3. Is the desire evil?

When God creates Adam and Eve, it is clear that He knows them better then they will ever know themselves. Is not the artist aware of the substance of his work? The creative act follows the knowledge of that which will be created. God had decided to create humanity in His image, and with that knowledge, He fashioned Adam and Eve. Mankind is created on the foundation of being known by God.

It is clear that Adam and Eve knew God. He had spoken to them, given them commands, and they had listened. God had observed Adam and knew him well enough to see his incompleteness without a covenant partner. There was a relationship between God and man. So when the serpent is working his deception, what is his method? The questioning of God's loving knowledge.

The serpent gets Adam and Eve to question the very foundation of their existence by telling them that God does not know them well enough to know what they need. He tells them that the "tree of the knowledge of good and evil" will not be a source of death to them, but a source of secret knowledge. He says if they eat of the tree that they "will not surely die. For God knows that when you eat of it your eyes will be opened, and you will be like God, knowing good and evil" (Gen. 3:4-5). Adam and Eve were already created in the image of God. They were *like God*, but the promise of the serpent implied that they would *be* God. No longer rooted in being known by God, Adam and Eve sought to escape so they could know *as* God.

We see the poisonous effect that sin has on knowledge throughout all of God's Word. As Augustine said, the human condition becomes *incurvatus in se*, which means curving in on one's self. We internalize and become focused on rooting our knowledge in self-knowledge as opposed to God's knowledge. Abraham's attempt to outsmart Pharaoh in Egypt, the golden calf in the wilderness, David's scheming to cover up his sin with

Bathsheba, and Solomon's pursuit of wisdom in Ecclesiastes all show the futility, hollowness, and destruction that can result from a quest for knowledge apart from God. All human attempts at knowledge apart from God's knowledge come from the maddening endeavor of escaping the awful reality of being fully known. We are terrified of being fully known because with that awareness comes the reality that we are not our own.

Knowing someone, JI Packer argues, is "more directly the result of their allowing us to know them than of our attempting to get to know them."[2] To be known by God is to be saved in Christ. God makes us a partner in covenant and discloses Himself through His creation, His Word, His Son, and His Spirit. Being brought into relationship with God and being known by God assumes full disclosure or confession. In God, we are fully known, for there is not one piece of ourselves that remains ours when we trust in Christ. **All knowledge is revelation from God. All knowledge is given.**

Genesis 18:19 says, concerning Abraham, that God had "*chosen* him, that he may command his children and his household after him to keep the way of the Lord by doing righteousness and justice, so that the Lord may bring to Abraham what he has promised him." The Hebrew word that is used for "chosen" is the Hebrew word for "know." What God is saying about Abraham is that "he is known" or "I have known him." When the Word of God speaks of our "being known" by God it is not saying that God is merely aware of our existence, but that God has chosen us for intimacy with Him. **Whenever our quest to know God is rooted in our being chosen, or known by Him, it will lead to worship, obedience, and mission.**

So is knowledge forever broken? Apart from Christ the human mind degenerates in the pattern described in Romans

---

[2] J.I. Packer, *Knowing God*, (20th anniversary ed. Downers Grove, Ill.:InterVarsity Press, 1993), 35.

1:21-23, "For although they knew God, they did not honor him as God or give thanks to him, but they became futile in their thinking, and their foolish hearts were darkened. Claiming to be wise, they became fools, and exchanged the glory of the immortal God for images resembling mortal man and birds and animals and creeping things."

In our case, the passage above could read, "For although they knew about God, they did not honor him as God or give thanks to him, but they became futile in their thinking, and their foolish hearts were darkened. Claiming to be reformed, they became fools, and exchanged the glory of the immortal God for arguments resembling passion, concepts being substituted for truth, and theology without worship and mission."

In Christ, our knowledge is restored but not made complete. We presently "see in a mirror dimly," but one day we will see "face to face." We now "know in part, but then we "shall know fully, even as [we] have been fully known" (1Cor. 13:12). Paul's pursuit of knowledge is rooted in being fully known by God. Long before the Apostle Paul, the Psalmist found opportunity to celebrate being fully known by God in Psalm 119.

The Psalmist begins by proclaiming the beauty of being known by God,

1   O LORD, you have searched me and known me!
2   You know when I sit down and when I rise up;
     you discern my thoughts from afar.
3   You search out my path and my lying down
     and are acquainted with all my ways.
4   Even before a word is on my tongue,
     behold, O LORD, you know it altogether.
5   You hem me in, behind and before,
     and lay your hand upon me.
6   Such knowledge is too wonderful for me;
     it is high; I cannot attain it.

He can't help but worship over the fact that God has *known* Him, or chosen Him. Remember that when it said that God knows someone, it often means something deeper than knowledge of one's existence. The Psalmist is thrilled that God has searched for him and chosen him for salvation. This deep knowledge that God has of His people is too great for the Psalmist, and he continues:

> [17]   How precious to me are your thoughts, O God!
> How vast is the sum of them!
> [18]   If I would count them, they are more than the sand.
> I awake, and I am still with you.

The thoughts and knowledge that God has of his people lead the Psalmist to say, "I awake, and I am still with you." Every morning the Psalmist wakes up is another opportunity to be with God—and God knows him. The Psalmist wants the Lord to continue to search and know him, for he says:

> [23]   Search me, O God, and know my heart!
> Try me and know my thoughts!
> [24]   And see if there be any grievous way in me,
> and lead me in the way everlasting! [3]

The Psalmist is overwhelmed with the knowledge that God possesses of His people. He realizes that he knows very little about God in comparison, but even the tiny amount of knowledge he possesses overwhelms his heart. The Psalmist allows the knowledge of God to lead him to piety, which is the practice of Christian truth. He allows his identity to be shaped by God's knowledge of him.

---

[3] *The Holy Bible: English Standard Version.* 2001 (Ps 139:1–24). Wheaton: Standard Bible Society.

The Psalmist wants us to realize that true knowledge of God is not gained but is given. If our "knowing God" is true, it will lead to obedience and worship. The Apostle John goes on to speak of this in the Gospel of John and 1 John.

The Apostle John: True Christian Knowledge

One of the many things that the Lord is so gracious to reveal through the pen of the Apostle John is the relationship that should exist between knowledge and action. John appears to have a deep passion for knowledge that is practiced. It appears throughout all of John's writings—most explicitly in John 13 and 1 John.

In John 13, we see Jesus washing the feet of His disciples on the eve of His crucifixion. "Do you understand what I have done to you?" Jesus asks the disciples as He washes their feet. Jesus wants them to realize that He is giving them an example of how they are to live as servants in the world. Christ goes on to say, "If you *know* these things, blessed are you if you *do* them" (John 13:17, emphasis added). True Christian knowledge is not simply the accumulation of ideas, facts, and concepts. True Christian knowledge is God's truth applied to life. The blessing of Christ among the Christian community does not merely rest in the knowledge of truth but in the practice of truth.

In 1 John, the apostle continues to point us in the direction of true Christian knowledge. He consistently reminds us throughout the letter that true knowledge of God will produce fruitful worship and obedience. John says, "By this we know that we have come to know him, if we keep his commandments" (1 Jn. 2:3), and that "anyone who does not love does not know God, because God is love" (1 Jn. 4:8). This direct link between knowledge and obedience is precious to John because he has seen firsthand what the idea of "secret knowledge" can produce in the life of a church.

In this particular letter, John is writing to the church in Ephesus. The church was divided because of the emergence of some in the church who claimed they had a "true" or "secret" knowledge concerning Christ. They proceeded to claim that Christ was not truly God in the flesh. They claimed that the head appeared to be human, but had not truly become a man. They were denying the beautiful truth of God's incarnation. John saw it for what it was, false teaching, but on top of identifying the false theology, he showed the church that one of the outward signs of this false teaching was that it did not result in love for God's people and a lost world; instead it created arrogance and division.

What would John's words to the young and reformed be? Do we walk around as if we possess a secret knowledge? Does our knowledge of God produce love and obedience to God's commands? **If we are going to claim that we know God intimately, by His grace, then that knowledge should be working in and through us to produce lives that are marked by the loving obedience that comes with truly knowing God.** The Bible never commends a detached or abstract knowledge of God. Knowing God is deeply rooted in living in obedience to His commands. The Bible never confines knowledge to the information of the mind alone; instead, it destroys the false division between the heart and mind by promoting a "working knowledge."

John Frame says that, "the knowledge of God is a heart-knowledge...all knowledge of God enlists all our faculties, because it engages everything that we are."[4] If we are content with living in the world of ideas, keeping our so-called "knowledge of God" in our thoughts, then we have not truly come to know God.

---

[4] John Frame, *The Doctrine of the Knowledge of God*, (Phillipsburg, N.J.: Presbyterian and Reformed Pub. Co., 1987), 322-323.

John Calvin

It would be foolish to write a book dealing with reformed theology and the stumbling blocks that are along its path without talking about John Calvin. Calvin was a French man who began by pursuing a career in law, but after experiencing a miraculous conversion, he was forced to flee France due to religious persecution. The Lord directed him towards Geneva where, after an unusual encounter with a man by the name of William Farel, he lived and served for the rest of his life.

Any picture of Calvin that pulls him out of the context of pastoral ministry immediately fails to deliver an accurate representation of the man. Calvin was a pastor, and when we examine his theology, we must always keep in mind that a pastoral heart fueled all that Calvin wrote and said.

Calvin's crowning literary achievement was the *Institutes of the Christian Religion*. It is the premier systematic theology of the Reformation, and the first two sections are titled "Knowledge of God the Creator" and "Knowledge of God the Redeemer." Calvin begins this great work by saying, "Nearly all the wisdom we possess, that is to say, true and sound wisdom, consists of two parts: the knowledge of God and of ourselves."[5]

For Calvin, knowing God was of supreme value because Calvin desired true *piety*. What is piety you might ask? Calvin calls piety, "that reverence joined with love of God which the knowledge of his benefits enjoins."[6] **Piety is the loving worship and obedience that is produced when a person truly knows God.**

Calvin does not have in mind some Gnostic conception of sinless perfection, nor does he have in mind a separation from the world. When Calvin encourages piety he is encouraging

---

[5] Jean Calvin and Ford Lewis Battles, *Calvin: Institutes of the Christian Religion*. (Louisville, Ky.: Westminster John Knox Press, 2001). 35.

[6] Ibid; 41.

Christians to know God as opposed to merely knowing *about* God. When we know God, we will be shaped by His revelation and will lead lives of obedience and worship. To repeat all that Calvin said about knowing God would be exhaustive—that is what the *Institutes* is entirely about. However, I want to point out that Calvin truly believed knowing God would, "not only arouse us to the worship of God but also awaken and encourage us to the hope of the future life."[7] For Calvin, simply knowing about God is not sufficient, for if our knowledge of God is genuine, worship and hope emerge as the fruit.

Truly knowing God does not just provide the Christian with piety, it also combats man's prideful self-interest. As Calvin points out, God's truth requires us to seek, "the kind of knowledge that will strip us of all confidence in our own ability, deprive us of all occasion for boasting, and lead us to submission."[8] True Christian knowledge leads us to ask the question, "What does the Lord require of you but to do justice, and to love kindness, and to walk humbly with your God?" (Micah 6:2).

Knowing God is not the accumulation of arguments, facts, and concepts that we use to elevate ourselves above "the rest." When we believe that we have gained knowledge of God and that somehow we have risen above those lesser, simpler minds to contemplate the divine, Calvin reminds us, "For who even of slight intelligence does not understand that, as nurses commonly do with infants, God is wont in a measure to 'lisp' in speaking to us? Thus such forms of speaking do not so much express clearly what God is like as accommodate the knowledge of him to our slight capacity. To do this he must descend far beneath his loftiness."[9]

---

[7] Ibid; 62.

[8] Ibid; 242.

[9] Ibid; 121.

True knowledge of God is given, not gained, by a God who descends far beneath His loftiness in order to speak to us as a mother to an infant. Still feel proud of your knowledge?

Straight from the pen of Calvin, we are made aware that our knowledge of God is given to know God and to make Him known. If it is used for any other reason, it merely becomes a form of Gnosticism that assumes that when Paul asks "For who has known the mind of the Lord, or who has been his counselor? Or who has given a gift to him that he might be repaid?" (Romans 11:34), there is one who can answer, "I have," apart from Christ.

The sad irony for those who take their knowledge of God into hoarding and hiding is that when they come before God, He will say, "Depart from me for I never *knew* you" (Matt. 7:23).

Being Known

So how do we put to death the pitfall of becoming like the Gnostics in our knowledge? How can we pursue knowing God without hiding ourselves from a world that rejects Him?

We must see that the greatness of God is not because He has given us the ability to know but that He has given His people the gift of being known. Only when our identity is rooted in being known by God can we approach or pursue knowing God. We must realize that, "If our attempts to discover God's ways are dissociated from a spirit of reverent worship, what we are seeking will remain hidden from us and the task to which we have been assigned will be left for others to accomplish."[10]

When we realize that as sons and daughters of the King we are known by God, we will not be satisfied with the

---

[10] Gerald Bray, *God is Love: A Biblical and Systematic Theology*, (Wheaton, Ill.: Crossway, 2012), 26.

superficial satisfaction of lording our knowledge of God over others. Resting in Christ allows us to know Christ as He is to be known: the great Savior, the true Sabbath, the image of the invisible God, and the perfect sacrifice. The cry of, "It is finished," on the cross of Christ is freedom to reject all of the exhaustingly hollow attempts at self-justification, including secret knowledge, for the strong foundation of Christ's atoning work.

Being known by God allows us to pursue knowing God deeply without defining our faith by what we can grasp. When Paul contemplates the sovereignty of God in Romans 8-11, does he end up frustrated that complete knowledge evades him? Absolutely not! He ends up singing a song! Romans 11:33-36 says, "Oh, the depths of the riches and wisdom and knowledge of God! How unsearchable are his judgment and how inscrutable his ways! For who has known the mind of the Lord, or who has been his counselor? Or who has given a gift to him that he might be repaid? For from him and through him and to him are all things. To him be glory forever. Amen."

Paul has just spent close to four whole chapters discussing the mystery of God's sovereignty in His plan of salvation. This whole teaching and reflection leads him to rejoice in song. Does our knowledge of God lead us to sing of God's greatness? If we don't find ourselves worshiping as we reflect on the glory of God, then we are not gazing at God's glory but some object of our own making. As my father has always reminded me, "Deep theology will lead to deep doxology."

How are you using the knowledge that God has graciously given you through His Word to worship Him? Do you feel worship and a desire to obey well up within you when you meditate on whom God is?

God gives knowledge to propel worship and missions. John Frame, in his wonderful book *The Doctrine of the Knowledge of God,*[11] argues that all human knowledge has a normative, situational, and existential perspective. Knowledge of God's norm or standards, knowledge of our situation or context, and knowledge of ourselves all work together to comprise how we know God. This means that when we encounter God's revelation, His norm, we look at our setting and ourselves in order to understand how that knowledge of God is applied.

The head, heart, and hands should all be affected as we come to know God. Our mind should be shaped by the knowledge about who God is and what He has done, our heart should respond in worship, and our hands should respond in obedience and mission. If worship and missions don't spring from the Christian mind, then it doesn't matter what you know, you have missed the point of God's truth.

Frame argues that, "Human knowledge of God is covenantal in character, as all human activities are. Knowing is the act of a covenant servant of God. This means that in knowing God, as in any other aspect of human life, we are subject to God's control and authority and confronted with His inevitable presence. Servant-knowledge is a knowledge about God as Lord and a knowledge that is subject to God as Lord."[12] Our human knowledge of God occurs in covenant relationship with God. Our quest to know God is undertaken as we enter into a relationship with God as Lord over all of life.

So true knowledge of God is rooted in being known (saved) by God so that we can grow in knowledge of who God is and what He has done in order to live that out. Is this how you treat knowing God? Is your knowledge of God rooted in His gracious saving knowledge of you? Do you desire to meditate deeply

---

[11] John Frame, *The Doctrine of the Knowledge of God*, (Phillipsburg, N.J.: Presbyterian and Reformed Pub. Co., 1987).

[12] Ibid; 40.

on who God is and what He has done? Are you living a life of worship to the glory of the God who has revealed Himself to you?

IN BRIEF

It is not wrong to desire to know God, but that quest to know God must be grounded in the truth that we may only come to know Him because He has revealed Himself to us. The fruit of this true knowledge of God will be seen in our lives through worship, obedience, and mission. The young and reformed movement will have to work diligently to put to death any idea that we have found a special knowledge reserved only for a precious few. Knowledge of God is not gained; it is given.

FURTHER READING

The Doctrine of the Knowledge of God by John Frame
Institutes of the Christian Religion Book I and II by John Calvin
Knowing God by JI Packer

Surrogate Christianity

5

In the digital age, Christians have a near-unlimited supply of resources from some of the most gifted teachers, preachers, and evangelists of our day. We can podcast an Anglican from England, a Presbyterian from New York, a reformed Baptist from Dallas, a charismatic Calvinist from Maryland, and an edgy, non-denominational Spurgeonite from Seattle.

The writings of these God-ordained men are now supplemented with audio, video, and interactive Internet Q and A's. All of these are blessings that technology has afforded us, and for the international church (a collection of local bodies with limited resources and materials), they are a gracious gift from God for their encouragement, education, and training. But as we have already seen, the sin that exists in the human heart can take God's blessings and twist them to be an escape from the present state of our Christian lives.

This pitfall of the young and reformed crowd hits home in a special way for me. Out of all the pitfalls discussed in this book, this is the one that I still habitually stumble into.

Two things have happened in this messy business of the Christian faith and the 21ˢᵗ century:

- There has been a subtle, hidden reintroduction of personal allegiance to gospel preachers (Paul-Apollos-Cephas 1 Cor. 1-4)

- The immense amount of resources across a palette of communication mediums has resulted in the young and reformed pitfall of vicarious sanctification, or surrogate Christianity

You may be confused, so let me briefly explain before we dive into deeper waters. **There is an imitation of godly leaders that is holy, and there is an idolatry of godly leaders that subverts their personal ministry and our personal worship.** We hear a sermon about the supremacy of Christ preached by a passionate and charismatic communicator, and we, through surrogate spirituality, believe we possess the same passion. We learn buzz words, body language, voice inflection, and hot topics in order to somehow claim the devotion and worship to Christ we see embodied in a leader for ourselves. We can be drawn into platforms and missions that are not our own and that don't show themselves in our context.

This is incredibly dangerous because it leads to a dependency on the communication abilities of godly men seeking to serve their congregations. This can result in a spiritual laziness as we consume the product of hours of prayer, study, and reflection done by others. It can also lead to an unwillingness to be taught by those godly men in our local congregations that may not have the platform of those we podcast, hear at conferences, or read.

Not only has this technology led to idolatry but also to a discontentment and disconnect between the believer and the local church. Many have decided that they would rather podcast a great communicator and listen to cutting edge worship music rather than bind themselves to a local expression of the Church. Most churches do not have the dynamic presentation that these larger churches possess. This is not to fault large churches, but when people who serve in small churches connect with the digital content of a larger church, they immediately have what the selfish soul desires: the ability to check out when the local presentation is not as dynamic or the communication is not as articulate.

We must seek out a holy imitation, not a religious idolatry. To do this we need to search out what a holy imitation is, see how idol culture creates idle culture, look at the life of John Knox, and devise a plan to practice a holy imitation.

A Holy Imitation

The fingerprints of those who have influenced our lives are all over us. When we start to examine who we are, we will inevitably end up looking at a long list of people who the Lord used to mold us. As I look at my life, I can see a line of godly men and women who labored to form me into the man I am today.

Who has influenced you? Write their names down. Is it a family member or friend? Is it a pastor or theologian? Is it an artist? Is it an author or professor? I encourage you to write the names down and thank God for using them to influence your life. The first step to a holy imitation is acknowledging that you have been influenced, that you are not an island unto yourself, and praising God that He was gracious enough to use these faithful people to accomplish His purposes in your life.

Listen to what the author of Hebrews 13:7 says, "Remember your leaders, those who spoke to you the word of God. Consider the outcome of their way of life, and imitate their faith."

The author of Hebrews is giving us an outline of how we are to treat the godly leaders in our life. The author challenges us to: 1.) Remember 2.) Consider 3.) Imitate.

First, you are to "remember your leaders." Any leader? No, only "those who spoke to you the word of God." Not all leaders are given the same seat of honor in the Kingdom of God. Those who spoke to us the Word of God are those who have given us that which is supremely valuable. We do ourselves a disservice if we limit this group to merely those in vocational ministry: preachers and pastors. There are many that were faithful to speak the Word of God to me who were never involved in preaching or pastoral ministry. We are to remember these people, so who are they? Maybe a Sunday school teacher has influenced you, maybe a pastor, or maybe John Owen or D.A. Carson? Remember them and thank God for the work He accomplished through them.

With the abundance of resources that the young and reformed have at their disposal, it can become increasingly difficult to pinpoint who has influenced you. To know who those people are allows you to become careful that you don't attempt to mimic them.

Secondly, you are to "consider the outcome of their way of life." The young and reformed should be careful that we don't too quickly exalt the work of any one man. For example, have you considered the Servetus affair that Calvin was involved in? Sure, Calvin's theology is rich and beautiful, but have you carefully examined the mistakes he made? Time tends to illuminate the mistakes that leaders make, so we must be careful that we don't lift up our leaders prematurely. If we dismissed every leader who made mistakes, we would be left without anyone to imitate. Instead, we are called by Scripture to "consider the outcome of their way of life." We should consider the outcome of our leader's lives and imitate the best parts of who they are.

For example, there are many leaders among the young and reformed who God is using in mighty ways, but the best among these leaders would caution you to watch your imitation carefully, for they are but men being sanctified by the grace of God. Because of the fatherlessness of this generation, the young and reformed are full of young adults who are looking for a leader. Let's be cautious in who we allow to shape our lives so that we don't make idols out of these leaders.

Finally, the author of Hebrews challenges us to "imitate their faith." A leader worthy of imitating will leave you desiring more of God and less of them. If you consistently find yourself leaving sermons, lectures, or worship services thinking to yourself, "That preacher is so cool, funny, and/or smart," then either the leader is self-exalting or you are looking for an idol to bow before. Because there has been an emphasis placed on the importance and work of godly leaders among the young and reformed, there is a temptation to look past the failures of our leaders because they hold to "our theology." We can look at Calvin and ignore Servetus or look at Luther and ignore his derogatory comments against the Jews.

Spurgeon said, "We may follow the man as far as the man follows Christ, but not an inch farther."[1] When you see a leader depart from the biblical picture of Christ, whether in deed, speech, or character, you must carry the good you have learned from that leader and continue to follow Christ. When Hebrews 13:7 encourages us to "imitate their faith," it is pointing us to that which is truly worthy of imitation: dependence on the grace of God. **We have many in the young and reformed who have become masters of imitating the personality of their leaders yet are empty because they have not imitated their faith.**

Who are you imitating? Whose name or movement have you branded yourself with? Have you considered the outcome of your leader's way of life? Are you imitating their personality or their faith?

These are important questions for this movement to consider.

---

[1] C.H. Spurgeon and Kerry James Allen. *Exploring the Mind and Heart of the Prince of Preachers*, (Oswego, IL: Fox River Press, 2005), 522.

Idol Culture Begets Idle Culture

Across Christian history, there has been a temptation to elevate the teaching or leadership of one person to the exclusion of others faithful to the gospel. **When preferences become standards, they become poisons that stir division and discord among the family of Christ.** This is not a new phenomenon.

In 1 Corinthians 3, we find the Apostle Paul addressing division among the church in Corinth. Various forms of pride and immorality had created a breeding ground for factionalism and division in the church, and Paul rebukes them by asking, "For while there is jealousy and strife among you, are you not of the flesh and behaving only in a human way? For when one says, 'I follow Paul,' and another, 'I follow Apollos,' are you not being merely human?" (1 Cor. 3:3-4).

The church in Corinth was divided among many things, but Paul thought it important enough to focus in on the division among preferred servants of God. The body of Christ in Corinth was split among those who preferred the ministry of Apollos and those who favored Paul. What separated the ministry of these two men? We will never know precisely, but it is safe to say, given what Paul says concerning the manner in which he came among the church in Corinth, that it had something to do with the speaking style and communication abilities between the two men. Is this beginning to sound familiar?

How often have you heard someone say regarding a preacher, teacher, or pastor, "He's good, but he's no _____." Fill in the blank. There is no doubt that God uses the gifts He distributes according to His sovereign grace in different ways, but Paul is quite clear when he says, "What then is Apollos? What is Paul? Servants through whom you believed, as the Lord assigned to each. I planted, Apollos watered, but God gave the growth. So neither he who plants nor he who waters is anything, but only God who gives the growth. He who plants and he who waters are one, and each will receive his wages according to his labor. For we are God's fellow workers. You are God's field, God's building" (1 Cor. 3:5-9).

Favoring certain servants of God over others is similar to rejecting the perfect T-bone steak set before you because of the plate it is on. **Your preferences are petty, and they poison the delight you should have in the object they were meant to point to.** Do you dismiss the work of God in your life because it isn't branded with the personality of your preferred leader or movement?

In the Corinthian church, this preference for leaders had been a disguise for all sorts of sin. It had the mark of spirituality, but it covered up a selfishness and immorality that was running the church into the ground. This was because *idol* culture creates *idle* culture.

The Book of Judges starts off with the death of Joshua, Israel's faithful leader, who helped to lead God's people into the Promised Land in the wake of Moses' death. Joshua was not perfect, but he was faithful. How do the people honor Joshua's death? The author of Judges tells us that "there arose another generation after them who did not know the Lord or the work that he had done for Israel" (Jud. 2:10).

Israel forgot their leaders, failing to consider their way of life or imitate their faith. Instead, they chose to "do what was evil in the sight of the LORD and served the Baals. And they abandoned the Lord, the God of their fathers, who had brought them out of the land of Egypt" (Jud. 2:11-12). In forgetting the faith of their leaders, they opted for idolatry instead of imitation. From this idolatry emerged a culture that was idle. They had been led by Joshua into the Promised Land and continued their conquest of the land. However, when they abandoned the Lord, their progress was not only stopped, but also reversed. Because Israel abandoned the Lord, "the anger of the Lord was kindled against Israel, and he gave them over to plunderers, who plundered them. And he sold them into the hand of their surrounding enemies..." (Jud. 2:14).

When God's people abandon the worship of the Lord for the worship of creaturely things, they will become a hollow shell of what they were created and set apart to be. God judged the people of Israel because of His fierce love for them, and we see a clear example of God's judgment in the raising up of Deborah to judge the nation of Israel. God had ordained that men would lead his people, but the sinfulness of God's people had left a nation without any men to lead. The raising up of Deborah to judge the nation was a sign of God's great anger with His people.

The judgment of God upon Israel is a sign to the Church that He will not share His glory with any other. For those of you who have made idols out of leaders, you are no different than those who would worship Baal. The young and reformed must learn how to remember, consider, and imitate without creating a culture of idolatry in the life of the Church.

John Knox

John Knox is a wonderful man to look towards when drawing a line between idolatry and imitation. Roland Bainton said, "Knox felt toward [Scotland's] idolaters as Elijah toward the priests of Baal."[2] John Knox was born between 1505 and 1514 in Haddington, Scotland. We know very little of Knox's early life, but he emerged as a follower of the preacher George Wishart around 1544.

Knox actually carried a broadsword and acted as bodyguard for Wishart. The Scottish authorities were working hard to

---

[2] Quoted in Douglas Bond, *The mighty weakness of John Knox*, (Orlando, Fla.: Reformation Trust Pub., 2011), Preface, Paragraph 1.

suppress the spread of the Reformation in Scotland, and Wishart was a major target during this persecution. After Wishart was killed for his faithful preaching of the gospel, Knox took up the mantle of his leader and began to preach Christ.

Knox was eventually exiled to Geneva where the French Reformer John Calvin welcomed him. Knox worked closely with Calvin, and Douglas Bond says that "throughout his ministry, Knox considered Calvin his spiritual father, and he sought the counsel for the Genevan Reformer in correspondences. So influential was Calvin in Knox's life and faith that when he lay dying, he asked his wife to read Calvin's sermons on Ephesians to him."[3] Knox would call Geneva "the most perfect school of Christ on earth since the days of the apostles."[4]

Knox followed and imitated Calvin in many ways, but he was not subject to the authority of John Calvin. In regards to Knox's opinions about civil government and the objection that a church might reject "a magistrate who enforces idolatry and condemns true religion,"[5] Calvin suggested that Knox should rethink his opinion in this area, and Knox refused this counsel. Even though Knox felt that in Geneva he was in "the perfect school of Christ," he still felt a burning desire to bring the gospel and his leadership back to Scotland.

So, what do we say about Knox? We say that he remembered Calvin, he considered his way of life, and he imitated his faith. He did not absorb Calvin's personality—in many ways he appears to be less calculating and strategic than Calvin. He did not live vicariously through Calvin's calling, opting to return to Scotland instead of remaining in Geneva. He did not strive for

---

[3] Ibid; Location 243.

[4] Ibid.

[5] Quoted in Douglas Bond, *The Mighty Weakness of John Knox*, (Orlando, Fla.: Reformation Trust Pub., 2011), Location 242.

Calvin's platform, and he was not primarily a theologian. It's clear that writing for the Reformation was a secondary matter for Knox. He sought to bring all of Christ to all of Scotland, and he strived for a holy imitation of Calvin. Had Knox brought the glory of Calvin back to Scotland, there would never have been revival there, but since he brought the glory of Christ to his country, we have the great outbreak of the Scottish Kirk (church) that produced such a wonderful work of God in that country.

Imitate Me, Imitate Christ

Have you ever watched a little girl playing dress up in her mother's clothes or a little boy with his book reading in his father's leather chair? As a child I remember watching my grandfather drink black coffee, so I drank my coffee black until I acquired a taste for it. How did you imitate your parents? How have you patterned your life after those you have followed? Don't just read the question; answer it.

We are imitators. We were created in the image of God (Gen. 1:27) to cultivate and subdue the earth. God created, and we were to use what God had created to create so that we might imitate the perfect creative act of God. We were created to imitate.

In my second year of studying philosophy at Dallas Baptist University, I was encouraged to read Aristotle's *Poetics* for a class on the study of beauty. Towards the beginning of this classic work, Aristotle writes, "Imitation is natural to man from childhood, one of his advantages over the lower animals being this, that he is the most imitative creature in the world, and learns at first by imitation."[6]

Aristotle applies this principle of imitation to the study of art, but it is precisely because humanity possesses this instinct

---

[6] Aristotle, Rhetoric; *Poetics*, (Modern Library ed. New York: Random House, 1954), 226-227).

to imitate that we find ourselves looking to imitate our leaders. Don't trust Aristotle? What about the Apostle Paul?

Paul says in 1 Corinthians 11:1, "Be imitators of me, as I am of Christ."

It is a bold thing to challenge others to imitate you. When you tell others to imitate you, you are asking them to have their lives shaped by the very thing that has shaped you. Paul is clear that there are two fundamental identities in life: in Adam or in Christ. If you are interested in investigating these identities, take a look at 1 Corinthians 15. Our identities, whoever we are "in," shape who we are and how we live.

By the grace of God, Paul finds himself in Christ, and he calls us to join him in this identity. Paul is not looking for us to imitate his gifts, his personality, or his weaknesses but to look at him and see what resembles Christ and imitate that.

Christians must not be guilty of joining a personality cult.

The young and reformed must be careful that we don't elevate the personalities, gifts, passions, and platforms of certain leaders above the mission of God in the person of Christ. At the risk of abusing his wit, we should remember yet again what Spurgeon said, "We may follow the man as far as the man follows Christ, but not an inch farther."[7]

We have been imitating since we were children, but sin fractured our desire to imitate. We now imitate the wrong things, and when we begin to imitate the right things, we can make idols out of creatures. So, how do we imitate well?

We remember those who spoke to us the Word of God. We consider their way of life, and we imitate their faith. We give special priority to those leaders who point to Jesus Christ in word and deed. We thoughtfully reflect on the character, conviction, and courage of these leaders; looking for any fault that we may

[7] C.H. Spurgeon and Kerry James Allen. *Exploring the Mind and Heart of the Prince of Preachers*, (Oswego, IL: Fox River Press, 2005), 522.

avoid. We then imitate the best part of who they are: their faith in God.

When we listen to our leaders—when we read their books or go to their conferences—"we follow them as far as they follow Christ and not one inch farther."

Will you join me in pursuing a holy imitation?

IN BRIEF

The young and reformed movement must be cautious that we follow our leaders only as far as they follow Christ. In order for us to practice a holy imitation of those leaders "who spoke to us the word of God" (Heb, 13:7), we must: remember them, consider their way of life, and imitate their faith. In the celebrity culture of the global west, we must constantly evaluate the posture of our heart before the leaders in our lives.

FURTHER READING

The Mighty Weakness of John Knox by Douglas Bond
Technopoly by Neil Postman

God in a Straitjacket?

6

Imagine that you are strapped into a straitjacket. You are capable of moving, but you are held back by a force greater than yourself. This feeling of inability is maddening, especially when you have a desire or hope to accomplish a purpose that you are being held back from.

Calvinists at this point are looking at the chapter title and thinking, "How dare he?" If there is one thing that a young, reformed individual is confident in, it is that they are not subtracting from the glory, the will, or the sovereignty of God. But they often are. Let me illustrate. In the youthfulness of this current resurgence, we have young men and women who will quickly profess that God is completely in control, that He is sovereign, but what they really mean is that God is all-powerful.

Omnipotence is the word we use when we mean to say that God is all-powerful. To say that God is all-powerful is to say that He is completely free to do all which is in keeping with His character. Often, God's power is challenged with the question, "If God is sovereign over everything, how do we have any freedom?" Horton answers, "Because God is freedom, such a thing as freedom exists and can be communicated to us."[1]

---

[1] Michael Horton, *The Christian Faith: A Systematic Theology for Pilgrims on the Way*, (Grand Rapids, Mich.: Zondervan, 2011), 261.

To say that God is sovereign is to say that He is Lord. God is a person, and His power is not some "impersonal force to be manipulated by human ingenuity. He has his own purposes, his own standards, his own delights and hatreds. He acts on his own initiative, rather than merely responding to events."[2] God's power is exercised through His sovereignty. When God acts, His infinite power works through His complete reign over all creatures to accomplish His perfect purposes.

It is rare to find an individual who genuinely believes and trusts in what they are saying when they say God is sovereign. If He is sovereign, there is nothing He cannot command of us. The thought that God has complete power is comforting, but the thought of God as sovereign can be quite terrifying. It leaves us subject to the will and authority of another. Often, we take God's omnipotence and make it synonymous with sovereignty in an effort to be able to wield His power without being subject to His authority. **Trusting in God's sovereignty flies directly in the face of our sinful nature, which longs for human autonomy, for radical freedom.**

When a young and reformed guy sees a tsunami hit the coast of Japan, he wants to immediately throw up the Calvinist flag and start speaking of the sovereignty of God. But when his heart is locked into Internet pornography, he will quietly dismiss the sovereignty of God over his purity. When the young and reformed woman is asked about gender roles, she will profess that she is a complementarian and that the man should be the leader of the home, but when she begins to doubt that God has a husband for her, she will place herself in compromising positions to gain love. **We want God to be all-powerful, but we don't want him to be sovereign. If God is merely all-powerful, we can control, manipulate, and compartmentalize His power, but**

---

[2] John Frame, *The Doctrine of God*, (Phillipsburg, N.J.,: P&R Pub., 2002), 25.

if He is sovereign, then He uses His power in keeping with His will and desires, not ours.

Still don't think this is a problem that has found its way into the renewed interest in Reformed theology? Ask those around you who subscribe to the sovereignty of God what their prayer life looks like? Ask yourself, "If God truly is sovereign, then why do I not labor diligently in prayer?" The Puritans were not satisfied with some divine power to be controlled or explained. Instead, they magnified the sovereign God who could and would be faithful to accomplish all His perfect purposes. In *The Valley of Vision*, we hear the voice of one who has been humbled by the truth of God's sovereignty, "O God whose will conquers all, There is no comfort in anything apart from enjoying thee and being engaged in thy service...I rejoice to think that all things are at thy disposal, and it delights me to leave them there...So shall I wait thy will, pray for it to be done, and by thy grace become fully obedient."[3]

The young and reformed must be careful that we don't tie up God's sovereignty in a straitjacket by claiming His power for our own ends. We have to ask, "Is God sovereign, and if so, what does His sovereignty mean for us?" Take a look at Augustine's story and figure out whether or not we want a sovereign God.

Is God Sovereign?

The ink has almost run out in attempting to answer the question of God's sovereignty. It appears to be a topic that has come up in the midst of every significant movement in church history. Augustine debated Pelagius, the Arminians contested Calvin, Spurgeon fought against the moderate Baptists, and now the young and reformed ask the question to the post-modern.

---

[3] Arthur Bennet, *The Valley of Vision: A Collection of Puritan Prayers and Devotions*, (Edinburgh: Banner of Truth Trust, 1975), 5 and 15.

Many different answers and solutions have been offered to solve the question. Deists suggest that God, while all-powerful, is not able to affect (or is indifferent to) the course of the world He started. Open Theists have argued that God does have authority, power, and knowledge, but He "takes risks and *jeopardizes* his own sovereignty in order to engage in historical interactions with created reality."[4]

Molinists have argued that while God possesses complete knowledge of every possible world that could exist, He does not control the future (although He does Lord over or determine the present). Theological compatibilists argue that God is sovereign and that people are not "constrained or compelled in their actions, but what they do flows unimpededly from their wants, desires, preferences, goals and the like."[5]

When we look to the Word of God regarding the question of His sovereignty, the name of God will inevitably emerge as a significant point in the discussion. *Yahweh* is the self-revealed, covenant name of God in the Bible. In Exodus 3:14, when Moses asks for God's name, God says, "I AM WHO I AM." The name Yahweh is translated into the word "LORD." While "LORD" does not communicate the fullness of God's revelation, it is how we seek to understand who God has revealed himself to be. So, when God reveals his name to Moses, He places His Lordship as central to His identity. From this, John Frame argues that, "the name of God, the name by which he wants his people especially to remember him forever, is Yahweh or Lord."[6] The word "LORD" appears in the NIV over 7000 times and mostly refers to God or to Christ.

---

[4] Clark Pinnock, *The Openness of God: A Biblical Challenge to the Traditional Understanding of God,* (Downers Grove, Ill.: InterVarsity Press, 1994), 125.

[5] Paul Helm, *The Providence of God,* (Downers Grove, Ill.: InterVarsity Press, 1994), 67.

[6] John Frame, *The Doctrine of God,* (Phillipsburg, N.J.,: P&R Pub., 2002), 21.

To say that God is "LORD" is to say that He is in authority, or possesses control, over His creation. Sovereign is the word we use to describe God's all-powerful nature working in relationship with His creatures. Gerald Bray insightfully remarks, "logically speaking, it is difficult to say that 'sovereignty' is a divine attribute because it has no meaning apart from creation; it is a relational term that is more meaningful to us than it is to God as he is in himself."[7] Bray is saying that God's sovereignty is what we call the going forth of His power, knowledge, and will in accomplishing His purposes and desires in His creation.

To say that God is sovereign is not equivalent to saying that God is all-powerful because "it is not simply that God is capable of doing whatever he wants to and cannot be hindered in this by any other power in the universe (omnipotence), but that he controls everything and rules his world directly (sovereignty.)"[8] **So God can and will do whatever He wants.**

Psalm 115:3 says, "Our God is in the heavens; he does all that he pleases." The verse assumes that God can do whatever He pleases and makes it explicit that not only is God capable of doing what He wants, but He is intent on accomplishing His purposes and designs. Not only is God capable, but also He plans on accomplishing His purposes for His pleasure. This is a God who is radically God-centered. John Piper demonstrates in the *Pleasures of God* why this is a beautiful truth. When we talk about God's sovereignty, "the point is that God acts in sovereign freedom. His acts do not spring from the need to make up deficiencies but from the passion to express the abundance of his delight."[9] When a Christian truly believes in the all-powerful

[7] Gerald Bray, *God is Love: A Biblical and Systematic Theology*, (Wheaton, Ill.: Crossway, 2012), 142.

[8] Ibid; 143.

[9] John Piper, *The Pleasures of God: Meditations on God's Delight in Being God*, (Rev. and expanded ed. Sisters, Or.: Multnomah Publishers, 2000), 52.

nature of God, He is declaring that, "God does all that he pleases by his power. This is what we mean by sovereignty—God's power always makes way for his perfections to be expressed according to his good pleasure."[10]

Often, God's sovereignty is debated in the face of salvation and tragedy. Rarely is God's sovereignty (the demonstration and action of His power) questioned in the face of blessing and abundance. It is easy to pay lip service to God's sovereignty when we are in a comfortable season. However, in the Bible we see God's sovereignty at the foundation of countless harsh realities. The story of Job is no small testament to the fact that God was at the center and in complete control of Job's testing. When we examine the cross of Christ, we ask, "Who killed Jesus?" Isaiah 53:10 says, "It was the will of the Lord to crush him..." and Acts 2:23 says, "this Jesus, delivered up according to the definite plan and foreknowledge of God, you crucified and killed by the hands of lawless men."

Although it is easy to claim God's sovereignty and control over blessing, we must realize that God's sovereignty is not relegated to that which is pretty and convenient. At the same time, God's sovereignty is framed by His goodness. God does bring difficult and trying seasons of suffering into our lives, yet He did not exempt Himself from this suffering. Christ endured the greatest affliction of God's sovereignty on the cross. Jesus Christ was the only perfectly innocent sufferer, and it was the will of the Lord to crush Christ on behalf of His people. **God's sovereignty is covered, like all of God's attributes, in the loving blood of the Son.**

The answer to the question, "Is God sovereign?" is yes. God is completely sovereign. God is Lord; He is in complete control and possesses complete authority over His creatures.

---

[10] Ibid; 53.

Right now, many of those who count themselves to be among the young and reformed are nodding along. You agree with me right? So what? What does God's sovereignty mean?

What Does it Mean that God is Sovereign?

To say that God is sovereign is to say that He is Lord of all. God does not just possess a power that is held back or restrained from working things according to His glorious purposes; He possesses complete authority and control. God's sovereignty means, as said in the *Westminster Larger Catechism*, "God's works of providence are his most holy, wise, and powerful preserving and governing all his creatures; ordering them and all their actions, to his own glory."[11]

God's authority and control in His decrees and actions extend over all of creation. He has not only composed the music of life but conducts every instrument with His perfect purposes. It means that all of creation is subject to the Lord, and "he is before all things, and in him all things hold together" (Col. 1:17). God's power is not a thing to be wielded by any man, for He is the "head of the body, the church" (Col. 1:18). He is in control and possesses all authority. Although we might desire to use His power for our ends, God will not relinquish His Lordship.

God's sovereignty is not pointless. He is controlling and ordering the universe with a purpose: His glory. God is, as we saw in the last section, God-centered. If God were not highest in His own affections, He would be unrighteous for He would be placing a lesser thing above Himself. God would be an idolater if He did not prize Himself above all else. The heavens declare the glory of God (Psalm 8). The Word of God leads us to reflect on the glory of God (Psalm 119). Jesus says in the garden that His

---

[11] Geerhardus Vos and G. I. Williamson, *The Westminster Larger Catechism: A Commentary*, (Phillipsburg, N.J.: P & R Pub., 2002), 44.

purpose was to bring glory to God (John 17). The Father glorified Jesus after His death and resurrection (Philippians 2). God has orchestrated the world for His glory. God exercises authority and control for a glorious purpose, the exaltation of God.

Having seen that God is sovereign, we become aware that, "there is not a square inch in the whole domain of our human existence over which Christ, who is sovereign over all, does not cry: Mine!"[12] This means that God is using all things: human salvation, politics, disaster, life, weddings, and funerals to orchestrate a symphony for His glory. God possesses everything and is using it all for the glory of His name. This is central to the Christian worldview because if Christ is Lord, or sovereign over all things, then all things can be used for the glory of God. The truth of God's sovereignty, the Lordship of Christ, liberates and frees all of life from an artificial divide between the sacred and the secular. Because God is sovereign, the work of the stay at home mom becomes an act of worship equal to the task of the preacher who stands in the pulpit. The engineer and businessman have a calling to glorify God in their workplace as the worship leader glorifies God in leading the church in song.

God is sovereign over your money, and He is calling you to not buy into the idol of consumerism that our culture has lifted high. God is sovereign over your purity, and He is calling you to pursue holiness in your private and public life. God is sovereign over your eating and drinking, and He desires that you not twist what He has made clean by being a glutton. God is sovereign over your purpose, and He is asking you to die to self and pick up your cross and follow him.

If God is not Lord over all, He is not Lord at all.

---

[12] Abraham Kuyper, "Sphere Sovereignty," in *Abraham Kuyper: A Centennial Reader*, ed. James D. Bratt (Grand Rapids, MI: Eerdmans, 1998), 488.

Augustine and God's Control of Our Lives.

Augustine is often left out of the reading plans of the young and reformed. Though he can be forgotten, Augustine's life and thought helped to shape the key leaders and ideas that emerged during the Reformation. Why should you care about Augustine? John Piper puts it this way, "the glory of God, however dimly, is mirrored in the flawed lives of his faithful servants. God means for us to consider their lives and peer through the imperfections of their faith and behold the beauty of their God."[13]

Augustine was an early church leader who was born in 354 AD. He lived the first 31 years of his life apart from Christ but experienced salvation in July of 382 AD. After his conversion, Augustine went on to be a major player in the formation of Christian theology, specifically the doctrine of the trinity and the truth of God's sovereignty in salvation. During his time as the Bishop of Hippo (396AD-430AD), he served his people and the church at large as the great defender against the three prominent heresies of his day: Manichaeism, Donatism, and Pelagianism.

It is a work of God's grace that Augustine was brought to salvation, let alone that he became one of the most significant leaders in the history of the church. His journey of grace is chronicled in Augustine's autobiography *Confessions*. It is a wonderful devotional autobiography that leaves the reader almost unable to discern where Augustine's writing ends and where his singing begins. The story is told from his point of view, long after his conversion, and in it we find the great story of God's sovereignty demonstrated beautifully.

In *Confessions*, we find that Augustine, before God saved him, was caught in the clenches of a fierce lust. Augustine's

---

[13] John Piper, *The Legacy of Sovereign Joy: God's Triumphant Grace in the Lives of Augustine, Luther, and Calvin*, (Wheaton, Ill.: Crossway Books, 2000), 37.

sin longed for the immediate and selfish gratification that accompanies sexual immorality, and his awareness of being caught in the grasp of this unconquerable sin led him to be a vocal proponent for the sovereign work of God in salvation. He says, "How sweet all at once it was for me to be rid of those fruitless joys which I had once feared to lose...You drove them from me, you who are the true, **the sovereign joy**. You drove them from me and took their place, you who are sweeter than all pleasure, though not to flesh and blood, you who outshine all light, yet are hidden deeper than any secret in our hearts, you who surpass all honor, though not in the eyes of men who see all honor in themselves...O Lord my God, my Light, my Wealth, and my Salvation."[14]

Augustine was sitting underneath a fig tree when he heard a voice chanting, like that of a child, "Pick up and read, pick up and read."[15] Augustine then hurried to where he had left a copy of the bible, and he "seized it, opened it and in silence read the first passage on which his eyes lit: 'Not in riots and drunken parties, not in eroticism and indecencies, not in strife and rivalry, but put on the Lord Jesus Christ and make no provision for the flesh in its lusts.'"[16] Augustine was converted by the sovereign and mysterious work of a Savior who is willing and able to save those He has set His love upon.

Before Augustine was brought to salvation in Christ, he had been drawn into the thought of Plato. Plato argued that "god" was all-powerful, but completely transcendent, meaning that he was not concerned in the affairs of the creatures. Plato's "god" is not only all-powerful, but he is apathetic to the affairs of humanity. Plato's "god" was powerful enough to save Augustine

---

[14] Augustine, *Confessions*, (Oxford: Oxford University Press, 1998), 155.

[15] Ibid; 152.

[16] Ibid; 153.

from the tangles of his sin, but he did not have the authority or desire to save Augustine from his self-destruction.

Augustine realized that the Triune God of the Bible had found him and delivered him from "fruitless joys," and in this deliverance, Augustine was given "the sovereign joy," who is God Himself.

After Augustine was saved, he went on to become one of the great defenders and spokesman for God's sovereignty in the work of grace. Speaking out against Pelagius (an early church heretic), Augustine argued that God's work of salvation is not constrained by man's will, but instead, man is free only in the sense that he is free to sin. Man cannot freely lay down his sin and choose Christ. Augustine argued this from the Bible but also from His own experience. **Having tasted of sovereign grace, how could he be satisfied with a faulty gospel?**

In many ways, Augustine helped to fuel the Reformation. Luther was an Augustinian monk in the Catholic Church who was led back to Paul's doctrine of justification through Augustine. Calvin quoted Augustine more than any other theologian throughout his *Institutes of the Christian Religion*. Augustine, like Calvin and Luther, was not satisfied with an omnipotent (all-powerful) deity; **he needed and desired a sovereign God who was not only able to accomplish the great work of salvation, but willing.**

In speaking of God's grace in Christ, Augustine asked, "Is it the case, then, that in order to find their way to the help of God, men run to God without God's help?"[17] Augustine's answer is, "by no means." He continues, "great indeed is the help of the grace of God, so that He turns our heart in whatever direction

---

[17] William Placher, *Readings in the History of Christian Theology*, (Philadelphia, Pa.: Westminster Press, 1988), 117.

He pleases."[18] Spoken as one who knows his dependence on God for salvation.

The young and reformed crowd should look to Augustine as an example of the despair of omnipotence when divorced from the sovereignty of God. Omnipotence is of no use in saving and sanctifying if God is not completely sovereign. **Let us not be impressed with an all-powerful God unwilling to exercise His great power. Instead, let us stand in awe of an all-powerful God who is intent on accomplishing His purposes.**

Do We Really Want God to Be Sovereign?

I often run to the historic catechisms and confessions for comfort, and Question 28 of the *Heidelberg Catechism* helps in asking, "What advantage is it to us to know that God has created and by His providence does still uphold all things?"[19] The answer the catechism provides reminds us that, "we may be patient in adversity; thankful in prosperity; and that in all things, which may hereafter befall us, we place our firm trust in our faithful God and Father, that nothing shall separate us from His love; since all creatures are so in His hand, that without His will they cannot so much as move."[20]

When we ask what it means that God is sovereign, we see that it means that God is in control and has authority over every created thing. Not only is God in control; He is powerful enough to accomplish His desires and plans for the purpose of bringing glory to Himself. This means that God is in control and authority over our salvation, our holiness, our money, our purpose, our

---

[18] Ibid.

[19] Joel Beeke, *The Three Forms of Unity: Heidelberg Catechism, Belgic confession, Canons of Dort,* (Birmingham, AL: Solid Ground Christian Books, 2010), 76.

[20] Ibid.

families, our friends, our hobbies, and every other possible dimension of our lives. Do we really want God to be sovereign?

There is no room for debate on whether God is sovereign or not, but are we going to rest and trust in His sovereignty or spend the rest of our lives attempting to hide from God's presence in God's world? The Bible only presents us with two options: we suppress the truth that God is our glorious Savior and King, or we rest in His sovereign grace. So, what's it going to be?

When we first encountered Psalm 115:3 in this chapter, we read that, "Our God is in the heavens; he does all that he pleases." This led us to examine the sovereignty of God, but we must not forget the Psalm that this verse finds itself in. Psalm 115 is preaching the hope of salvation in God. The great comfort in knowing that God does all that He pleases is seen when we realize that it His great pleasure to shower love and grace upon His people. Psalm 115 talks about the hollow nature of idols; they are powerless and without personality, and the psalmist urges the people of Israel to "trust in the Lord! He is their help and their shield...the Lord has remembered [them]; he will bless [them]" (Psalm 115:9-11).

The idols that Israel so often abandoned God to worship were hollow and powerless. In turn, they left those who worshiped them hollow and powerless, for "those who make them become like them; so do all who trust in them" (Ps. 115:8). If idols are powerless and can never deliver on the false promises they make, why would you be comforted by their emptiness? In the face of these idols, the writer pushes our vision towards the true God who, "does all that he pleases." **We should desire a God who is completely sovereign because He has both the power and the desires to accomplish good for His people.**

God's sovereignty is the promise that His steadfast love and faithfulness will conquer our sin and apathy. If God were not sovereign, there would be no hope of salvation, for we would never choose God apart from His choosing of us. If God were not sovereign, there would be no joy in trusting a God who was bound by a straitjacket. If God were not sovereign, our prayers would be vain hopes to a god who was always trumped by the will of the world. If God were not sovereign, the hope of His return would be clouded by the circumstances of a broken world.

Even though God's sovereign plan and will may place us in circumstances that demand radical sacrifice, perseverance, blessing, or suffering, we stand on the firm foundation of God's goodness and His promise to accomplish all things for His glory. May God bring us to the point where every discussion of God's sovereignty begins with, "Not to us, O Lord, not to us, but to your name give glory, for the sake of your steadfast love and your faithfulness!" (Ps. 115:1).

We who make up the ranks of the young and reformed must be cautious that we do not undermine the Lordship of Christ as we talk about the sovereignty of God. **When we become flippant with such a rich and beautiful truth as God's complete authority and control over creation, we can grow numb to the marvelous wonder of the God who acts in creation.** Are we as a movement living lives of holiness that demonstrate God's sovereignty over our private lives? Our thoughts? Our hearts? Are we so consumed with the sovereignty of God that we are obedient to the call of sacrificial living? Are we so consumed with the sovereignty of God that we are willing to pursue the lost with the same ferocity with which God pursued us?

God is sovereign. He is Lord. There is nothing that He cannot ask of His people.

IN BRIEF

The young and reformed must be careful that they do not settle for an all-powerful god and call him sovereign. The God of the Bible is omnipotent (all-powerful) and sovereign (in control and authority) over all of His creation for the purpose of glorifying Himself. We cannot name and claim God's power merely over the areas of life that we desire to give God Lordship. Instead, we must see that God is Lord *over* all, or He is not Lord at all.

FOR FURTHER STUDY
John Frame, *The Doctrine of God*
John Piper, *The Pleasures of God*
Augustine, *Confessions*
Valley of Vision

Conclusion

Are we there yet?

Maybe you have heard this familiar phrase emerging from the back of your car as you are traveling. As a child, when I would ask my parents this question, they would always reply, "15 minutes." My parents understood that for children, 15 minutes was as long as an hour, and our minds would have imploded had they told us we were six or eight hours away from our destination.

So, are we there yet? Have we arrived? Are we in the golden age of the church? There should be a holy longing, a righteous discontentment that plagues the heart of every Christian. We should always realize that this world is still groaning, and we must refuse to be ignorant to the darkness around us. Even as we sit reading the books of godly leaders from church history, we hear them saying, "All is not right...all is broken...but Christ is coming...He is coming to restore." Our King is coming. "Behold, [He is] making all things new" (Rev. 21:5).

Paul says in 1 Corinthians 13:12, "For now we see in a mirror dimly, but then face to face. Now I know in part; then I shall know fully, even as I have been fully known." It would be the height of presumption (and ignorance!) for us to claim that we have finally arrived. We will look back on this period in the history of the church and praise God for His faithfulness in light of our negligence and ignorance. For that really is what being reformed is all about, isn't it? Being people who throw themselves at the feet of God and say, "Not my will be done, but Your will be done" (Luke 22:42).

As we have spent the past pages examining pitfalls along the path to becoming young and reformed, you may have grown discouraged as you realized that there is much "reforming" left to be done. You may have had your suspicions confirmed, and now you realize that the young and reformed movement is hopeless apart from the grace of God. You're right.

The young and reformed movement is absolutely hopeless, apart from the grace of God. The sooner we remember that profound truth, the sooner we will realize that it will not be our theology, our method, our trendiness, our knowledge, or our gifts that will bring revival, but the great work of our great God!

As I researched and wrote this book, I was led to repentance, and there were people I had to go and ask forgiveness from. There were pastors, professors, friends, and family who I, in my recklessness, had wounded by my pride and arrogance. I hope these chapters have led you to confession, repentance, worship, obedience, and mission. Who do you need to go and ask forgiveness from? What wonderful truths of God's Word are you letting sit in your mind while your heart and hands go hungry? Are you being faithful to your local church? Have you made an idol out of an idea, a leader, or a movement?

There is grace for you. Paul asks in Romans 7:24-25, "Wretched man that I am! Who will deliver me from this body of death? Thanks be to God through Jesus Christ our Lord!"

Semper Reformanda was one of the principles of the reformation, and it meant "always reforming." Let this book challenge you to examine your life before God's Word and ask Him to restore the broken parts of who you are. Then, when you are in the midst of desperation for His grace, go out and proclaim the beautiful love of the Savior.

Lord, come.

Join the Conversation?

Have a comment, question, or complaint about the book?

Join the conversation on Twitter by using the hashtag #pitfallsjbo. The author will be joining in on the discussion frequently.

You can find Kyle Worley on Twitter @kyleworley.

If you have any speaking requests you contact Kyle Worley through his blog at www.thestrife.com or facebook.com/thestrifeblog.

www.ingramcontent.com/pod-product-compliance
Lightning Source LLC
Chambersburg PA
CBHW032007040426
42448CB00006B/515